7

ANOTHER COUNTRY TALK

ILLUSTRATED BY VALERIE WARREN

ANOTHER COUNTRY TALK

J.H.B. Peel

ROBERT HALE · LONDON

First published in Great Britain 1983

ISBN 0 7090 1282 9

Robert Hale Limited
Clerkenwell House
Clerkenwell Green
London EC1R 0HT

Photoset by Photobooks (Bristol) Ltd.
Printed in Great Britain by
Redwood Burn Ltd, Trowbridge, Wilts.
Bound by W.B.C. Bookbinders Ltd.

Contents

Other books by J.H.B. Peel include:

POETRY
Light and Shade
Places and People

ESSAYS
Country Talk
More Country Talk
New Country Talk
Country Talk Again
Country Talk Continued
Latest Country Talk

TRAVEL
Portrait of the Thames
Portrait of the Severn
Portrait of Exmoor
Along the Pennine Way
Along the Roman Roads of Britain
Along the Green Roads of Britain
An Englishman's Home
Peel's England
All Over Britain
People and Places

1

All the Year Round

Another year begins. Twelve months lie ahead, all with their own quirks and customs. Were I asked to choose an attribute from each month, I would say of January that it is the season when we first notice the lengthening daylight. Shortly before Candlemas a cottager can dig his garden at an hour when Advent found him in darkness. The bleak mid-winter really does offer a guiding light toward the spring.

February is the month when countryfolk first notice the flowers. Among sheltered places in the south-west the snowdrops and primroses and Lent lilies shine in small clumps or in masses covering many square yards. On these Exmoor hills the lanes are bright with the celandines which Wordsworth thanked for

> Telling tales about the sun,
> When there's little warmth, or none.

March is the month when bird song ceases to be a whistling in the dark. Meredith's thrush vies with a blackbird, singing (as Edward Thomas reckoned)

> Twixt dawn and dusk, from half-past six
> To half-past six . . .

April reminds us that many parts of the kingdom are still a green and pleasant land. On St George's Day a haze shimmers above hedges while larches flaunt their vivid foliage. Meadows and lawns literally take on a new lease of life, compared with which their winter herbage was drab. April's green light confirms that spring has arrived.

May is the warmth when we once again feel warm, not merely tepid. Despite frost and gales during the early days the temperature can reach seventy-five degrees Fahrenheit. Even a

hill farmer casts the proverbial clout. Although the calendar claims that spring has not yet gone out, a countryman shares the mediaeval poet's belief that summer has at last come in.

June, says the calendar, is predominantly a spring month, yet the same arbiter has set Midsummer Day in June. The month's chief glory is a blend of colour and scent, from the red thorn and the white rose to the blue catmint and the yellow pansy. Buttercups and daisies dapple the meadows. Campions and nettle flowers speckle the lanes. June, in short, displays a fragrant rainbow, and most people choose it as the summit of summer's splendour.

I regard July as a marking-time month because the apples

and nuts are not yet ripe, and the corn is still uncut. Granted, the birds have lost their springtime voices, but the hours of daylight seem hardly to have dwindled, and a heatwave makes it difficult to believe that autumn is approaching.

During August, on the other hand, autumn becomes perceptible. We dine by lamplight, we watch the birds migrating, we detect the leaves turning. This is the month when old men recall the harvests of their youth . . . horse-hauled, pitch-forked, stooked and ricked; followed by a feast in the barn, with many songs and much drinking; and finally the slow walk home under a moon so huge that little children fancy they could leap thereon without the aid of space ships.

Like March (which has one foot in winter), September (with one foot in summer) marks a transition, for it is farming year's top-dead-centre, the moment when the piston is poised, ready to start a new cycle. Reaping has almost ended; ploughing will soon begin. At noon a shepherd sweats on the hills: at dusk he basks beside a fire. This is the season of 'mists and mellow fruitfulness', often beginning with a warm spell, usually ending with an equinoctial gale.

It is tempting to choose the fiery leaves as October's special feature. Seen against a blue sky, the woods achieve a beauty comparable with Cleopatra's, which never cloys nor loses its infinite variety. Even so, I choose a different fieriness because, for the first time since March, we need a fire all day and every day. On All-Hallows Eve we no longer pretend that summer still lingers.

November can produce an Indian summer, an Arctic blizzard, a bare-bough covert, a robin singing solo to the silence. Nevertheless, I suspect I am not alone in citing mud as the month's most conspicuous feature. So recently glistening with dew, the grass beside a field gate has been eroded by hooves that churn a green sea into a brown mire.

In December the spring seems as distant as the summer, yet many country-folk will say that the bleakness is cheered by the angel's 'glad tidings of great joy', inviting us to practise the good neighbourliness which John Clare observed among the villagers:

Wishing with smiles and spirits high
Glad Christmas and a happy year
To every morning passer by.

Myself, I would emphasize the Christmas enlightenment by choosing darkness as December's badge. Throughout Advent the lights are switched on at teatime and may have been burning since breakfast. A countryman sees the stars when he goes to bed and again when he wakes up. Bright days do occur, and never more dazzling than under snow; but the skies are often grey and sometimes black, as though the year were mourning its own decease.

Looking Forward

I hope that I am not the only one who in January finds it difficult to imagine what the trees look like in June. Certainly I am not the only one who either sits by the hearth or plods through the mud, remembering when the mud was dust and when the hearth was filled with ferns.

At the moment the weather is of a sort which invites a sarcastic reply when you bid the postman 'Good morning'. The logs fumigate the room. Rain trickles down the windowpane, like streaks of sullen candle grease. Gusts of wind slap a dead leaf on to the front door and then slip one underneath it, silent as a surreptitious Final Demand. Half-visible through mist, the trees resemble outworn besoms. In short, it is Cecil Day Lewis's season of dereliction:

In these our winter days
Death's iron tongue is glib . . .

At such times I open what we call the mind's eye, seeing a panorama of blue skies, green pastures, and water so still that the sun seems to have solidified it. Some people will regard the vision as escapism; others, as a retreat *pour mieux sauter*. In any event, certain forms of escapism are desirable, and to ignore them is foolish. Do we reject a dental anaesthetic, or a night's sleep, or a Strauss waltz? Surely not, for such things may relieve us from painful reality. Admittedly, the present prospect cannot be called painful, yet no one would find much pleasure in the claustrophobic mist, the creaking branches, and the lower part of hills whose summits are cloud-capped. Even while I look, the rain beats harder and louder, foreshortening a cramped horizon, as in Edith Sitwell's chiaroscuro:

> Still falls the rain,
> Dark as the world of man, black as our loss . . .

Turning from that murk, I see this page and on it these words, stealthily filling it while between the lines a picture emerges—coloured, melic, scanted, warm—transporting me from a wintry desk at noon into a Maytime garden at dawn. Already the sun is benign and will soon become hot. Blackbirds are singing a song that was learned in Eden long ago; almost nonchalant they sound, confident as a poet who masters his art *con amore*, neither needing nor heeding a newer vogue. Through the trees I see a skyline of wooded hills, dappled with hawthorn blossom. It is going to be another glorious day.

Now once more I glance up, and the vision fades. In its place come those rods of rain, those birdless branches, those thunderous gusts, and another fistful of leaves against the door, onto the windows, into the gutters, all over the lawn. One crow lumbers by, sometimes swerving on a try-again tack, sometimes plummeting as though it were a cumbrous lark, slowly making steerage way through weather that would tempt even the *Valkyrie* to put-about and make for any port in such a storm. With a shivering shrug I turn again to the inward vision, seeing a sandy beach which burns the soles of bare feet. The sun glares, yet no one complains. From mid-morning till late afternoon the holiday makers bask in the blaze while wavelets plash, seagulls mew, dogs bark, and somewhere a child calls 'Coo-ee!'. Everyone is either thinking or saying: 'If only it were like this all the year round . . . or even for three whole weeks.'

Now something sad has happened; something so real that it caused me to go into the hall, thinking a visitor had knocked on the window. Forcing the door open against the gale, I found spots of blood and a dead robin that had been hurled off course, either through misjudgement or because of infirmity. How roughly such so-called trivial incidents awaken us from comfortable illusions about a benign Providence. Nevertheless, like life itself, these lines go on, leading me to mountains that make a stranger envy the folk who sing of the Land of their Fathers. A shepherd appears, brown as bracken, old as Methuselah, wiser than Solomon. 'Hot it is,' he tells me. 'Almost too hot. But the lambs like it, mind.' Then, as he sweeps a wide arc with a horny forefinger, the pride of Cymry speaks: 'The trees on the mountains', he says, 'and the sun on the trees. A proper picture, eh? My grandson he hops off to Spain or somewhere, but I tell him, "God made Wales early on the Monday morning when He was full of bright ideas".'

Have you ever crossed Salisbury Plain while the wheat-fields surge like a molten sea, and the windows of a distant farm flash as if they were a lighthouse, and the walker needs to slake his thirst at every fourth mile? Have you ever reached the Spittal of Glen Shee while the turf is warm to touch, and everywhere the cuckoos pipe a cordial pibroch, *Cead Mille Failte*? Have you ever strolled through the Buckinghamshire woods at Little Hampden while the beaches are peerless in June's perfection? Have you ever watched the Northamptonshire harvesters while Cold Ashby melts its Saxon forename? Have you ever entered Worcestershire's Wyre Forest while the Severn shimmers like quicksilver far below, sweeping past Arley at apple-blossom time, lamb-loud and daisy-pied, with one old fisherman contemplating a sun-drenched float? Have you ever entered Great Tew—Lucius Cary's old Oxfordshire estate—while June goes down like a dauntless *Téméraire*, burnishing the thatch on venerable cottages, dappling the birds as they chant their Evensong, offering tranquillity to all who are in a state to receive it? Have you ever explored the zany lanes of Romney Marsh in Kent, on a day so still that you hear, or imagine you hear, the sea surging through the shingle?

Daydreams, you say? Certainly; yet even in January they are dreams that will one day come true.

Tones of Country Talk

'Hemmels weer hotchin' wi' haytimers.' There indeed is country talk, and although the spelling does not reveal the meaning of the words, it does suggest their sound . . . a difficult task, requiring not only a knowledge of language but also an ability to steer between too much and too little phonetic guidance. William Barnes, for instance, attempted an aural-visual reproduction of the Dorset dialect:

> The girt wold house o'mossy stwone
> Had woonce a bleäzèn kitchèn-vier
> That cook'd vor poor vo'k an' a squier.

An enjoyment of the poetry of those lines is stifled by the difficulty of pronouncing them, and the difficulty of pronouncing them is made even more laborious by the accents and apostrophes and diaereses. The result is a fair specimen of the kind of speech which many satirists and scriptwriters assume to be a *lingua franca* anywhere west of Basingstoke.

Thomas Hardy was more sparing in his phonetics. Thus, Joseph Poorgrass, a very shy man, liable to turn red in the face, utters only a minimum of Dorsetshire: 'Blushes hev been in the family for generations. There, 'tis a happy providence I be no worse.' In fairness to Barnes, however, we must remember that his own Dorset verses were intended primarily as reproductions of a dying dialect, whereas Hardy wrote for people who were concerned rather to enjoy a story than to enunciate a vernacular.

Meanwhile, we are left with 'Hemmels weer hotchin' wi' haytimers' . . . words, by the way, that were not written many years ago, in a book about Victorian rustics, but were spoken a few years ago (I still have the BBC recording of them, which I made in Northumberland). The speaker was a retired farm-hand, ninety years of age, who told me that in his youth the haymakers often slept in hemmels or sheds on the farm; as a result, the sheds were hotching or teeming with scythe-men.

Another of his recollections included 'A maid an' twa trugged th'auld peeal' (One or two of the girls carried the old or customary pail for milking cows) and 'A mort o' braw lads bided with feymeer' (Many of the sturdy youths lodged with the farmer).

When Daniel Defoe explored Northumberland two centuries ago he detected a quirk of country talk that is almost as noticeable now as it was then. 'Northumbrians', he reported, 'are distinguished by a shibboleth upon their tongues, a difficulty in pronouncing the letter *r*, which they cannot deliver, from their tongues, without a hollow jarring in the throat . . . This they call the Northumbrian *r*, and the natives value themselves upon that imperfection because, forsooth, it shows the antiquity of their blood'. Defoe did not explain why a slurred speech should connote a long lineage. He and the Northumbrians would have been on firmer ground had they cited the Cumbrian pronunciation of 'school' as 'skule', which resembles the sound now made by Danes whose ancestors colonized a large area of northern England. Some people trace the Northumbrian *r* to Shakespeare's Harry Hotspur, the headstrong son of the Earl of Northumberland, who was king of the north in all but name. Mediaeval chroniclers stated that Hotspur suffered a speech impediment, and history confirms that the northerners adored him as a hero; therefore, it is said, they imitated his speech, which may have slurred the letter *r*. Howard Pease, the twentieth-century historian, who lived at Elsdon in Northumberland, believed that the regional use of 'champion' as a synonym for 'splendid' arose because the northerners did indeed regard Hotspur as their champion against the London bureaucrats. The Elsdon villagers still have a Northumbrian *r*, yet at Allendale, only a few miles way, I found no trace of it. Puzzled, I consulted a linguist from Durham University, who modestly confessed that he, too, was puzzled. Why should one village retain the *r* while a neighbouring village has either discarded it or never adopted it? Has anybody ever examined the palate and vocal cords of those who do utter the *r*?

The tones of country talk symbolize a gradual merging of

dialects that were spoken during the Dark Ages, when a Suffolk farrier would have sounded almost unintelligible to a Roxburghshire shepherd, and both of them would have been incomprehensible to a Cornish miner. When Chaucer, a fourteenth-century Londoner, asked a Kentish housewife for some eggs, the woman remarked on his outlandish accent. During the Middle Ages the dialects coalesced to form a common language, though still with regional variants, so that the words 'they come' would in Cheshire be 'thai comis', in Hampshire 'he cometh', in Norfolk 'thei comen', and in Shropshire 'hi comen'. A few of the old regional words are still heard . . . 'slack' for 'valley' in Westmorland, 'master' for 'first-rate' in Devon, 'kurlik' for 'charlock' in Oxfordshire.

Regional dialects, then, can easily be accounted for; but what are we to make of the different accents which exist within the same county? Thus, a few veterans in Westmorland can tell whether an elderly farmer comes from Kendal or from Kirkby Lonsdale, yet those two places are scarcely a dozen miles apart. Less than twenty years ago, simply by hearing them speak, Claude Berry could tell whether people came from the west of Cornwall or from the east. As a large number of televiewing yokels would now say: 'Folks, it sure is kinda quaint.'

External Decorations

Since the wind bloweth where it listeth, and since birds and insects follow a comparable *laissez-faire*, the seeds of trees and flowers may be carried a considerable distance before they fall and take root and multiply. Thus it is that we sometimes see a solitary thorn, or a pool of primroses, in places where we would not expect to find them. At other times a line of beeches and a cluster of snowdrops will cause us to say: 'They didn't just spring up by chance. Somebody took the trouble to plant them.' One such botanical garden blooms each year beside a bridge over a small river in a combe near my house. Another—a few rhododendrons—stands on a fell above Kirkby Lonsdale in

Westmorland, miles from any occupied house. The riverside garden was planted by a smallholder for his own pleasure and that of the handful of farm-folk who follow the lane. The rhododendrons were planted to please a nobleman who built a shooting lodge on the isolated summit; both he and his lodge vanished long ago, but the rhododendrons abide, hardy as a perennial Ichabod. A similar planting has been made in my own fields, the story of which may seem worth the telling, less for its own sake than as a hint to other landowners, whether of a small patch or of a large park.

It all began when I first came to live here and discovered that the property contained many square yards of snowdrops, primroses, and the wild daffodils or Lent lilies which adorn North Devon like benign weeds. Unfortunately, one patch of flowers was hidden by an embankment near a derelict cottage (now demolished and rebuilt as a small woodshed-cum-stable). Another patch, likewise hidden by an embankment, could be seen only after walking across the field and then looking back. I therefore decided to dig up the flowers and to set them in the grass on one side of the drive leading to the house. Finding that no amount of uprooting seemed to diminish the areas of annual regrowth, I turned my attention to the other side of the drive, which is a typical Exmoor earthwork, about eight feet high and several feet wide, faced with stone and topped by a double row of beeches. So, whenever I looked up in January, I saw the first harbingers of spring peering down at me from the top and also from crevices between the stone. Before the snowdrops had faded they were joined by clumps of Lent lilies, and before the lilies had faded, out came the primroses, shining like yellow coins that had been scattered as largess, even as Stevenson scattered his thanks in the Cevennes.

As you may imagine, this floral redecoration was not accomplished in a day nor in a week nor even in a year. After ten years, finding that the original sites still produced flowers, I set about planting the residue on top of an embankment between the woodshed and the house; and there also in January I see the snowdrops which, unlike snowflakes, do not flinch from the sun, but are coaxed thereby to rise and shine. Likewise the

Lent lilies appear and among them another scattering of primroses, all visible from this desk, and all offering a wordless welcome whenever I walk up to the woodshed or count the sheep that keep the higher paddock in good heart.

As gardening, of course, the work was scarcely more than hard labour leavened with an eye for external decoration (to have aligned the flowers in regimental array would have mocked their natures), yet I cannot survey my handiwork without experiencing a trace of Coleridge's 'meek Sabbath of self-content,' for there were times when the planter was, or at any rate felt himself to be, as hardy as the perennials. Year after year the second week of January found me out of doors despite rain, mist, sleet, hail, and a wind that struck straight from the Steppes, rousing more noise than seemed possible in the bare-bough wood beside the garden. Gloveless and on my knees, I worked like a sedulous mole, separating every plant so that all might start again with a more or less equal chance of survival. Minuscule bulbs were set alongside others that had already flowered. Sometimes only a dozen were planted together; at other times twenty or thirty, each clump set deep enough to ensure a firm anchorage, and then packed with earth at the base. You will be surprised to discover how long it takes—how much of time and energy—to dig up one hundred plants, to carry them two hundred yards down a steep field, and then to re-establish them carefully. A whole hour may pass, and you seem to have achieved very little indeed.

As I say, it was a prolonged task, undertaken in many weathers, sometimes with zest, sometimes with dour determination, always with visible progress to spur me on. I have gone to it soon after sunrise while the ground was more like rock than like soil. I have been at it long after sunset while February's first thrush sang the day's last Evensong. Once or twice I worked in sunshine. Often I returned so caked in mud or so sodden with rain that I felt obliged to perform a semi-strip act before entering the house. But those days, those years, are past. From late January until mid-May I now reap the reward of labouring through many bleak winters, sharing Laurence Binyon's hope:

The seed is sown
And in the Earth I trust.

Unlike Quintus Flaccus, I may not claim that my own poems are monuments *aere perennius*, more lasting than brass; but I do claim that, long after I have been forgotten, the owner of these few acres of England will point to the flowers, saying: 'They didn't just spring up by chance. Somebody took the trouble to plant them.'

Ringing Down the Curtain

Sir Richard scarcely remembers when it was that he first engaged Mr Cosmo and another elderly actor to produce and take part in the annual charity pantomime at the Hall, but he believes that the fee was five guineas apiece plus board and lodging at a gamekeeper's cottage. Although the second actor is now too frail to travel, Mr Cosmo was invited to attend the latest matinée performance in the Tudor barn. Many children and adults enjoyed the show, together with a number of Sir Richard's personal friends.

Among the players was a village youth who, having won a RADA scholarship, had already made a promising professional start as Romeo and Hamlet, helped by Sir Richard . . . a debt which he repaid by performing in the pantomime, his role being to declaim some Shakespearian speeches that had been inserted among the adventures of Dick Whittington.

Mr Cosmo himself, arriving in his son's car, presented an impressive appearance. After a long period in moth balls, his fur-collared top-coat seemed no more than an old man's justifiable protection against the cold. At the end of the matinée, while the players were still assembled on the stage, Sir Richard made a brief reference to Mr Cosmo. 'A much-loved friend,' he said, 'familiar to us through many years, but now a member of the audience.'

Leaning on a silver-topped cane, Mr Cosmo rose to acknowledge the applause. He then drew a breath deep enough

to sustain the opening sentence of a peroration. 'My lord, ladies and gentlemen, I first appeared on the stage at the age of seven months, my mother having left me, not, as Dame Edith Evans so often remarked, in a handbag, but in a shopping basket which the leading lady was required to carry during act one. Like other well-reared children, therefore, I remained seen but not heard. Yet even if we exclude that premature and speechless debut, I may still claim to have served the Muse for more than sixty years.'

After a second deep breath he said: 'I see from the newspapers . . . or at any rate from one newspaper, the *South Shires Chronicle* . . . that I am, as the late Dan Leno would have said, billed to appear, though not to speak. Nevertheless,' here he looked hard at the young Shakespearian actor, 'I *shall* speak; not, indeed, to say I feel as though I had just heard the ghost of Sir Henry Irving, nor even as if Tree had just emerged from his immortal Green Room, but I do say . . . we have this evening sighted a star, risen, I am told, with the help of Sir Richard himself, and born in this village.' Suddenly he let go his stick, seeming no longer to need it. 'Ladies and gentlemen, when one's own star has faded and will soon be extinguished, is it not a fine thing, a noble thing . . . in a word, a good thing . . . to know that one does not leave the world to total darkness? I therefore felicitate my young friend, my heir and successor. May he tread the boards *laude cum magna*, which being translated means Encore, or, as dear Marie Lloyd would have said, Let's hear it again.' The old actor then sat down amid loud applause and some cordial whistling from children who were still wondering what on earth he had been talking about. Sir Richard patted his shoulder, whispering: 'Splendid! A far, far better thing than you have ever done before.'

Ten minutes later Mr Cosmo joined the select party of friends for tea in the Long Gallery, whence he gazed admiringly at the parkland shining like a green sea. Turning to the bishop, he said: 'For those of us who serve the Muse . . . and here I venture to borrow a Roman phrase . . . London is indeed *urbs et orbs*, the centre of the universe.'

'And yet,' the bishop began.

'How right you are,' Mr Cosmo continued, 'Another member of the profession, Irving himself, was likewise born and bred in the country. One of my . . . were you, by the way, ever on Romney Marsh?'

'Er, no,' the bishop admitted.

'But I was. One of my earliest memories is of the Marsh. I used to stay at an aunt's cottage there, almost within sound of the sea. In fact, I became a youthful Autolycus, a picker-up of considerable trifles, of dew on the meadows, of hay in the nostrils, of seedtime and harvest.'

'Shall you,' the bishop asked, 'retire there?'

'My lord, I *have* retired there, to my son's farm, only three miles from auntie's old cottage.'

'How very pleasant,' the bishop murmured. 'Kent, I believe, has been called the Garden of England.'

'Of England? Say rather, of Eden. Parts of it, I allow, have been marred, but the Marsh has not been marred. The lanes there are still peaceful, whereon, you remember, sundry gentlemen rode by, bearing brandy for the parson and 'baccy for the clerk.'

'Rye,' the bishop tried again.

'Rye, as you were about to say, is not in Kent. No doubt there are other beautiful places that are not in Kent. For me, however,' Mr Cosmo took a third crumpet, 'Kent is still the Garden of England, and tomorrow, God willing, I shall return to it.'

2

A Lone Survivor

One side of the unfenced road slopes steeply to a network of combes or interlocking spurs, a habitat of moorland sheep and red deer. On the other side of the road a track climbs a knoll from which you can sight the Atlantic and the Severn Sea, with Lundy Island looming like a granite pyramid. After a few hundred yards the track starts to descend, so that the encircling hills leave you alone in a land of coarse herbage, rocky outcrops, and treeless summits. No houses are visible, no barns, no buildings of any kind . . . only a few sheep which, until they move, might be taken for mushrooms. Having reached the brink of a barren ravine, the track suddenly alters course, crossing a stream via several stepping stones before toiling up the side of yet another ravine, though not this time a treeless one, for there—carried by the wind, perhaps, or by a passing bird—there, many years ago, the seed of a thorn tree fell and took root and prevailed against the wind and rain.

On first sighting the tree from a distance I marvelled as much at its loneliness as at its smallness, but as I drew nearer I saw that it was a sizeable tree, about five feet high; and when at last I stood beside it I marvelled less at its loneliness than at its gnarled and stunted appearance, almost entirely covered with grey-green lichen or moss. Rooted in crevices among rocks, the tree had evidently relinquished the struggle to grow upright against the gales, and had chosen to grow sideways, sending out branches parallel with the ground. At the time of that first sighting I did not halt to examine the tree closely, though I did glance back at it from the summit of the next hill whence it looked no larger than a shrub. Something about the lone survivor must have impressed me, because I often remembered it during the ensuing weeks. Eventually I returned there, marking the length of the roots that protruded like grey cables above the soil. I noticed also the angle of the branches, some pointing upward, some downward.

Nowadays I visit the tree several times a year, at all seasons and in all weathers. It really is a hardy perennial. Many of the branches are as distorted as an arthritic hand. The tips of the twigs are so brittle that even a slight pressure may snap them. In calm weather at this season the tree appears to be dead, but during wild weather it appears to fight for life. Even the thick lower branches shudder while the smaller ones quiver frantically. The sound of the wind is partly a sigh, partly a shriek, partly a snarl. Unlike this stunted specimen, many thorns attain a height of twenty or thirty feet, and instead of struggling along against an inclement climate they cluster companionably among hedges throughout southern England. The young shoots' pink tips may be seen as early as March, pushing aside the brown scales. The timber of a hawthorn is greyish brown, whereas blackthorns were named after their dark timber.

It was during a February gale that I feared the tree could endure no more and would topple and be swept downhill by the blasts. Since then, whenever I come within sight of it, I glance upward, wondering whether it has died or been uprooted. Several times I have been there when a gale forced me to turn my head in order to breathe. Twice—though only from a distance—I have seen the tree glittering under a façade of frozen snow. Once, when a sudden mist came down, I really did think the tree had been uprooted; but no, always it survives, steadfast as a ship riding a storm, bare-masted indeed and often listing, yet securely anchored above a sandy bottom.

In spring, when deciduous trees elsewhere are covered with new foliage, the thorn wears only a scanty garment, and some of its leaves are embrowned soon after they have unfolded. During such weather the sun shines from a cloudless sky; the grass grows apace, as green as the habitat allows; lambs bleat, hares bask, larks soar like a psalm, and all day long the cuckoos send an echo through the combe. The earth, in short, is like an infant Lazarus risen miraculously from the dead; but this thorn never does look young. It reminds me of Wordsworth's tree, concerning which, in a note to the poem, he quoted an exhortation from the Old Testament: 'Arise, arise . . .' But, as I say, the thorn remains half asleep despite the summons. In these dark days I often think of the tree, buffeted by wind and rain, coated with moss and a veneer of brine from the Atlantic. My own house, on the edge of Exmoor, receives more than enough rough treatment from the weather; how much rougher are the blows that afflict the thorn, alone on a hill nearly a thousand feet above the sea.

Although it may seem fanciful, I regard the tree as an example of fortitude in adversity. Even now, while I write, a gale is blasting its way over the hills, tossing up twigs, bending back branches, slamming gates, flattening grass, roaring and moaning and shrieking. With the mind's eye, therefore, I see the thorn, its branches trembling, its roots heaving. Then indeed the lone survivor resembles Wordsworth's:

> There is a Thorn—
> In truth you find it hard to say
> That it could ever have been young,
> It looks so old and grey.

Points of View

Standing in the young couple's garden we exclaimed: 'What a wonderful view!' Having said so again and again—six times, all told—we began to feel repetitive. Our hosts, however, did not think so. 'It was the view', the husband told us, 'that clinched the deal. I remember saying to Marion, "The house is at least a thousand more than we can really afford, but those mountains are worth a million".'

People whose windows overlook a beautiful countryside cannot keep on saying: 'What a wonderful view!' Unlike

Browning's thrush, they must eventually lose their rapturous response. As one whose home does overlook a beautiful countryside, I know very well that if I stopped and stared whenever I wanted to mow the lawn or to reach the lane, I would in the course of a single year spend several hours *not* mowing the lawn and *not* reaching the lane. Nevertheless, so far from breeding contempt, familiarity (in the sense of old acquaintance) may deepen a lifelong admiration. But what of the rapture? Is it recaptured whenever we open the door to admit the cat or whenever we shut the window to exclude the rain? Clearly not, for we are incapable of being, in Wordsworth's phrase, permanently 'surprised by joy'. We may, however, be occasionally surprised by an uprush of gratitude—even of astonishment—because we do indeed see beauty all around us, not simply during an annual holiday, but whenever we glance through the window, walk to the wood shed, or empty the ash-bin.

When I gaze from my window, or walk down the drive, I do admire the view, and sometimes I find that it reveals what may be called new novelties, of a kind which greeted Francis Kilvert in his Radnorshire parish: 'Familiar as this place is to me', he wrote, 'I am always noticing some fresh beauty or combination of beauties, light or shade, or a view from some particular point where I have been at some particular hour and under some particular circumstances.' I recall three such 'particular circumstances'. The first of them occurred during spring, when I stood in the garden, peering into the deep combe and seeing a mist there, floating above the stream; and when the mist had passed, a rainbow appeared, as though anchored in the stream itself. The second example occurred during autumn, when the rising sun touched the larches on a hill in the middle distance; for a moment I half believed that the trees were on fire. The third example occurred during winter, when a sunset imprinted the snow-covered meadows with patches of pink and blue shadows that sparkled like jewels on a bridal gown.

The widest views I ever beheld were from Slieve Donard in Ulster and from Ben Nevis in Inverness-shire. Although the former is less than three thousand feet high, it overlooks Snaefell on the Isle of Man and also the lighthouse at St John's Point in Scotland. Ben Nevis, of course, is Britain's loftiest mountain, more than four thousand feet among cloud and mist which occur so frequently that the widest vistas are seldom visible on more than six days each year. Choosing one such day, Seton Gordon sighted Skye and the Outer Hebrides.

I doubt that any British parsonage enjoyed a finer prospect than the one from the old vicarage at Firbank in Westmorland. The fells below the garden slope steeply to the River Lune and thence up again, high above Howhill and Sedbergh, capped by The Calf at two thousand feet. I remember also the panorama from an upper storey of the Colquhouns' home at Luss, showing Ben Lomond and the loch. I arrived on a pellucid May evening while the sun and the sky covered the water with a blue mantle whereon a white yacht glided, swanlike, silent and stately. Mountainous views are the widest, yet even at a thousand feet a hill may seem to be the roof of the world. I remember the prospect from the house which Mary Webb and her husband built on Lyth Hill in Shropshire. I remember the Channel and the Downs as seen from Firle Beacon in Sussex. I remember the Midland montage as seen from Combe Hill in the Buckinghamshire Chilterns, with the Cotswolds like a cloud bank on the horizon. More than once I have admired the Welsh coast and the Malvern Hills as seen from Dunkery Beacon in Somerset; the Lancashire Pennines, rising like another and a nobler world, as seen from the motorway near Manchester; and the Marcher country as seen from the heights above Broadway in Worcestershire.

At other times we may prefer a more intimate glimpse, as of the church and the inn at Sutton Courtenay in Oxfordshire; the salt-water creek at Pecuil in Cornwall; the seclusion of Toller Whelme (a church and two houses) in Dorset; the stream at Finchingfield in Suffolk; the cobbled square at Sheepwash in Devon; the miniature harbour at Silva near St David's in Pembrokeshire; the Cambridge 'Backs' when dawn gilds the daffodils; the riverside houses at Wivenhoe in Essex. Some people will prefer the quadrangular camaraderie of Bainbridge in Yorkshire, where a hornblower sounds curfew at dusk; or the canal and thatched cottages at Great Bedwyn on the edge of Savernake Forest in Wiltshire; or the dormer-windowed cottages at Bunyan's Elstow in Bedfordshire; or the mediaeval bridge beside a narrow lane at Geddington in Northamptonshire.

I can almost hear the rivals raising their voices on behalf of the mediaeval almshouses at Ewelme in Oxfordshire; the beech woods at Ashridge in Hertfordshire; the off-beat antiquity of Honington in Warwickshire, the village green at Piercebridge in County Durham; the weatherboarded cottages beside the Horse and Groom at Lamberhurst in Kent; the enviable isolation of Holy Island in (and sometimes off) Northumberland; the pastoral quietude of Tennyson's Somersby in Lincolnshire; the brick-and-flint cottages flanking the lane to the sea at Blakeney in Norfolk; the church and magpie parsonage, glimpsed across a lake, at Gawsworth in Cheshire; the ancient houses overlooking a pond at Lingfield in Surrey; and as many more as there are protagonists to proclaim them.

Love in a Mist

Happening to meet a stranger hereabouts, I remarked: 'A lovely day.' For several moments the man stared at me. 'Lovely?' he said at last, and walked away.

On reflection I decided that to call the day 'lovely' was not, after all, to misuse language, because the day's beauty really was lovable. Had I called it 'super' or 'smashing' I would indeed have erred, but to cavil at 'lovely' seemed both pedantic and unjustified. Second thoughts, however, suggested that the stranger had objected not to the way in which I praised the day, but to the fact that I had praised it at all. 'Yes', I told myself, 'he must have thought I was dotty.' Once again, though, I changed my mind, this time saying: 'I am *not* dotty. The mist *is* lovely, and so are those blurred trees, and the fields, too, shining with silver-grey moisture.' Having acquitted myself of slovenly speech, I resumed the enjoyment of weather that would have seemed depressing in November and disastrous in May, but was now acceptable if only because February had emerged from the darkest season.

Viewed through the mist, every object seemed either to loom or to lurk. Signposts did not stand still, but advanced with finger pointed, like an accusing counsel. The tops of trees appeared to be suspended in mid-air. Branches overhanging the lane came as a surprise, like a whiplash in slow motion, causing me to duck. Sometimes the grey pall was rolled back, revealing a field gate which, six seconds later, vanished with the breeze that had uncovered it. By muffling the various sounds and by deterring the creatures that made them, the mist heightened the stillness of winter in deep country, but it also revealed one exception to the rule. For example, a wood adjoins the house, and on the far side of the wood lies a lane, and on the far side of the lane a stream flows through a combe or steep ravine. On most days of the year this stream is inaudible from the house, but now it sounded quite loud. Standing in the upper field, high above the house, I peered down on the unseen combe, feeling somewhat as Keats felt when, having scaled Britain's loftiest mountain, he tried to see the famous vistas therefrom:

> Upon the top of Nevis, in a mist!
> I look upon the chasms, and a shroud
> Vaporous doth hide them . . .

Nevertheless, neither the mist nor the silence could put back the calendar. The catkins, the buds, the lengthening days . . . all the old signs were there, and each of them seemed new. Mist or no mist, birds were mating, and several species would soon lay their first clutch. Squirrels were abroad, taking the mild air. Lent lilies flowered alongside snowdrops (the first snowdrop in this parish was flowering on Christmas Day). Among these heights the lambs are seldom born until late March, but if I had walked a couple of miles downhill I would have heard bleating from the Captain's farm, where lambing starts in January.

During the afternoon I went out again, noticing that every object exuded moisture. The dry-stone walls glistened, the barbed-wire glistened, the paths and puddles and posts glistened. At a first glance you would have said that the only colours were pale grey, mid-grey, and dark grey; but in the lane the withered leaves of a beech hedge glowed fierily through the haze. Half a mile away Farmer Seymour was rounding up his sheep, man and dog being as mystified as Clare's:

> . . . blindfold they trace
> The plains that seem without a bush or tree,
> Whistling by guess the sheep they cannot see.

At the end of the day, about an hour before bedtime, the dog and I returned to the upper field. No moon was visible, no star, no cloud, no sky at all. I could not tell where the summit ended nor where the horizon began. Far below, the house sent up a faint glimmer from a chink in the firelit curtains. Even the dog seemed mesmerized by the stillness, wondering what had happened to owls, foxes, beetles, mice. After a few moments it started to rain, as though disproving Andrew Young's assertion:

> So thick a mist hung over all,
> Rain had no room to fall.

But this rain did fall; in fact, it fell so fast that within three minutes the dripping trees sounded like an endless line of people walking through the wood. Somewhere in the combe a sheep coughed, eerily human. Somewhere else a bird squawked and then, after a second false alarm, went to sleep again, leaving only the stream's indefatigable rumination, and the trees pattering the soil with moisture.

Even the most weatherwise countryman would have shaken his head if somebody had asked him to name the month; it might have been any time between November and March, as indeed it was, yet so much nearer to March than to November that, despite the mist, one could almost see the spring. Then the rain stopped, as unexpectedly as it had started, though the trees continued to patter last year's leaves. Instead of rummaging and sniffing, the dog kept to heel, still puzzled by the mist. When I turned, he gladly led the way downhill to the house. Peering through a chink in the curtains, I saw the logs burning, proof that winter does not end merely because we wish it to. For a few more moments I stood listening to the sound of imaginary footsteps through the wood; then—no stranger being present—I went indoors, saying to the dog: 'A lovely night.'

Engle-Land

East Anglia was originally part of *Engle-land*, the territory of the *Engles* or Angles who came from Slesvig. Nobody knows why the name 'England' was promoted from a regional to a national status. The kingdom might with equal justification have been called 'Daneland' or 'Juteland'. Instead *Englisc* became the name both a people and their language.

East Anglia comprises Norfolk, Suffolk, Huntingdonshire, and Cambridgeshire, to which some topographers may add parts of Bedfordshire. The region's varied landscapes elude a single classification. However, no one will deny that East Anglia is generally flat, predominantly agricultural, relatively dry, and at times bitterly cold. When Celia Fiennes reached Ely she shivered in the 'Sudden winds that rise like Hurricanes . . . The Bishop does not care to stay long in this place for his health . . .' Although the Romans drained several of the East Anglian marshes, it was not until the seventeenth century that a Dutch engineer, Cornelius Vermuyden, began the major reclamation for which he received a knighthood from Charles I. Even so, it would be wrong to regard the whole of the region as a fen. John Constable praised 'the beauty of the scenery, with its gentle declivities, its luxuriant meadow flats sprinkled with flocks and herds, its well-watered cultivated uplands, its woods and rivers, with numerous scattered villages and churches, farms and picturesque cottages . . .' Constable's regional patriotism was shared by his East Anglian contemporaries: Gainsborough, Ladbrooke, Cotman, Crome.

During the Middle Ages the region grew rich on wheat and wool and water (from Ipswich to King's Lynn the ports carried most of the nation's overseas trade). Then came the industrial or mechanized revolution and with it the cheap imported food which ruined many farmers. Once the wealthiest corner of the kingdom, East Anglia was slow to join the race for the bigger factories and faster speedways that have transformed Ipswich and King's Lynn into industrial hives.

East Anglia's small towns compile a splendid litany: Wisbech, Lavenham, Spalding, Woodbridge, Fakenham, Long Melford, Bury St Edmunds . . . all in their fashion have resisted the excessive 'development' which, in Joseph Conrad's words, 'obliterates the individuality of old towns under the stereotyped conveniences of modern life'. Conrad himself, arriving here as a Polish *émigré* who spoke no English, learned his seamanship alongside East Anglian coastal sailors. 'Gentle men', he called them, strong, upright, brave. Norfolk and Suffolk, in fact, are second only to Devon and Cornwall as slipways for famous mariners, of whom Nelson was one, Anson another, and Cloudesley Shovel a third. Any short list of East Anglian worthies must include the Pastons, Sir Thomas Browne, Bunyan, Porson, Coke of Holkham, George Crabbe, Fanny Burney, George Borrow, Edith Cavell.

A bird's eye view of East Anglia can do no more than rest briefly on a few personal memories . . . on Holt, for example, a lively little town with brick-and-flint houses, rubicund farm-folk, and the well-mannered boys from Sir Thomas Gresham's ancient school. Lavenham's mediaeval houses are famous, each one so crazily contoured that its roof and façade resemble a switchback. I think also of Flatford, asleep beside the Stour (except at tourist time). I think of Blakeney marshes, patrolled by booming bitterns; of Castle Acre Priory, a rose-red ruin on a green site above a blue stream; of Great Massingham, a cluster of thatched cottages and duck-paddled ponds; the Roman *Via Devana* at Cambridge; that other Roman road, Peddars Way, whose alpha and omega lies among sand dunes at Holme-next-the-Sea; and an even older road, the Icknield Way, from the Gog-Magog Hills to the West Country. Pleasant indeed is the wooded country near Sandringham House, a private residence, into whose gardens the Queen invites her subjects. Sheringham, too, is pleasant, a type of East Anglian Sidmouth, Victorianly well-bred; and Finchingfield likewise is pleasant, with riverside cottages and a lane to the church crowned by a cupola. I hope that Progress has not yet improved the lane to Alconbury Weston near Huntingdon, nor the lane (is it still unfenced?) from Thornage to Brinton.

But those are merely private memories. Other people may think of Barton Broad near Nelson's old school, or of Wivenhoe (there, too, the church has a cupola) with boats moored alongside bar parlours. Others, again, will remember the triforium at Peterborough Cathedral; Oxburgh Hall, towered and embattled, seat of the Bedingfields since the Wars of the Roses; the watermill overlooking the Bure at Horstead; Columbine Hall at Stowupland, an ancient manor house rising Venus-like from its moat; Hollesley they call it 'Hozeley') where Shingle Street is a track leading to shingle shores and a martello tower. Truly the list is legion: Elm Hill, that narrow lane in Norwich, flanked by Tudor houses; the shrine at Walsingham; the great barn at Copdock, where I used to put Farmer Pulham's horses over the sticks; Hales church, with a round tower and a thatched roof; Masefield's 'dirty British coaster' sighted from the place where Dunwich once stood; and the sandy seclusion of Norfolk's Breckland, where prehistoric settlers dug for flints in deep shafts.

Benjamin Britten set the East Anglian coast to the wind-swept music of *Peter Grimes*, Vaughan Williams evoked the gentler landscapes from *A Norfolk Rhapsody*. Gentle or wind-swept, many East Anglian scenes still justify Constable's avowal: 'I love even every stile and stump, every lane in the village.'

Getting into Hot Water

Quite a number of cottages still lack a bathroom. Until relatively recent times it was unusual to find a cottage that did not lack a bathroom. Even some of the parsonages lacked one. During the 1950s, for example, the bath at Charlecite Rectory in Somerset was in an attic, with a twenty-gallon oil drum rigged above a paraffin stove. The water had to be carried upstairs in buckets. Radstock Rectory, in the same county, lacked any bath at all.

This unhygienic *modus vivendi* would have appalled the Roman soldiers in Britain, who not only enjoyed but also expected to take a hot bath every day, even at small forts in remote places. There was a Roman saying, that baths and wine and women made life bearable. Nearly 2,000 years later some of our country hotels provided no such amenities.

In 1949, arriving at a small Cornish hotel after a long journey, I felt that hot water was a necessity rather than a luxury. The bath, however—used by all the guests—was so short and narrow that, so far from being able to lie down in it, I had to crouch, with my knees doubled up. The hot water flowed so slowly that the bath remained tepid throughout the operation.

Like the word 'racing', which has become a synonym for horse racing, the word 'bath' is now a synonym for a hot bath. Some hardy Britons take a daily cold bath, and during very warm weather many other people do the same. The best cold baths I ever took were at sea, while living in a boat in Cornish waters. On most mornings between May and September I stepped over the side, swam a few strokes and clambered on board; and since my clothes consisted of a pair of shorts and a naval cap, I could bathe several times a day without needing to waste time on undressing and then dressing. Against an absence of soap I set the fact that brine is itself a purifier.

How frustrating it can be, when a hot bath is laborious as well as unsatisfactory. Many years ago, I went as a non-paying pupil on a Hampshire farm that was lit only by candles and oil lamps. The family never bathed more than once a week. On bath nights the farmer's wife dragged a tin tub into the kitchen, filling it—no, pouring into it—a few inches of warm water. As it proved impossible to lie down, and uncomfortable to sit up, I stood and scooped the water over my head. Accustomed to a real bath every day, I eventually walked several miles to the nearest hotel twice weekly.

To be without any bath at all is indeed a hardship. The victim dreams about hot water, even as hungry men dream about rich food. Only once has this happened to me, at the end of a long day's march in mountainous country. On reaching the hotel, I was dismayed to find that it had been destroyed by fire, yet during the previous week I had reserved a room there. Fortunately, a gamekeeper appeared, who told me that a cottage, scarcely two miles away, provided bed and breakfast so thither I went.

The place looked clean, at any rate from the outside, and the elderly couple were evidently pleased to receive a guest, but when I asked for a bath the woman said: 'We haven't got one.' Alone at supper in the parlour, I would gladly have exchanged the cold meal for a hot bath. Nor was that all; when I was about to fall asleep a scratching sound came from the floor, and five seconds later a rat ran across the bed, uncomfortably close to my face.

Winter or summer, a bath is among the minor pleasures of life, especially for people living in the country, who take more exercise than townsfolk do, and submit themselves more often to the elements. Not without reason is a hot bath noted for its benign effect on our thoughts, even when the thoughts are fallacious. No doubt because of its acoustics, a bathroom has persuaded many people that they can sing like Caruso, or at least like Bing Crosby. Even A.E. Housman—a gloomy music-hater—even he may have hummed in his bath.

Was it not in a bath that Archimedes exclaimed: 'Eureka! The weight of a floating body' etcetera. Napoleon, they say, planned many famous victories while the steam circled warmly above his head. Not so Sir John Falstaff, whose reluctant ablutions were cold as well as muddy. 'Have I lived,' he cried, 'to be carried in a basket, like a barrow of butcher's offal, and thrown into the Thames?'

My own most memorable immersions occurred after a day's beagling. Returning home mud-stained and aching, how warmly I exchanged greetings with the log fire; how thankfully I removed the sodden clothes; how wearily, yet with what a sense of wellbeing, I tested the bath water; not too hot to enter, but temperate enough to wallow in, with the taps so adjusted that a constant trickle maintained the kindly sting. Sometimes—I confess it—I nearly forgot to wash myself, so blissful it was, doing nothing, thinking nothing, enjoying everything.

Afterwards, when I had changed into dry clothes, the log fire seemed to add flavour to the boiled eggs, the buttered toast, the sweet tea; and when, a few hours later, I retired to a warm bed, the effects of the bath were like those of a mild opiate. This evening, perhaps, you, too, will sing, or at any rate hum, the praises of a hot bath after a day in the open air.

3

Winter versus Spring

March is a month much maligned. That having been said, most people will agree that spring's arrival often seems unspringlike, except to cynics who regard it as very springlike indeed. Thomas Gray greeted the season optimistically:

> Beside some water's rushy brink
> With me the Muse shall sit and think . . .

Had Gray and his Muse sat beside a certain Exmoor river the other morning their thoughts would have been interrupted by large boughs careering pell-mell on the flooded water.

Even so, the month continues to be maligned. Stung by an east wind, we forget that March has sometimes soothed us with a southern breeze. Enervated by winter's longevity, we deplore the unconscionable slowness of its demise. Not content to see the snowdrops decline, we demand to watch the tulips bloom. We become disgruntled because the month fails to fulfil promises that were never made. March, in short, is a victim of our own impatience, which thinks only of spring's inclemency. The proverbial lamb, however, needs to be set alongside the lion, and from that juxtapose a third metaphor will emerge, a creature of roughness and gentleness, of hailstones and sunbeams, of anticipation and realization. In that mixture every country lane reveals winter versus spring. Bruised though they are, the daffodils gleam like polished trumpets. Primroses might be glow-worms in the grass. Lambs are loud calendars, incessantly reciting the date. Bluebells are silent calendars, stealthily surmounting the soil. Hares go boxing with rivals in an eternal triangle. Moles and shrews also fight, screaming angrily. At dawn and again at dusk the birds hold a resonant rehearsal for those summer days when the sun rises before the shepherd and when a robin's bedtime coincides with the cowman's.

Aroused from winter sleep, frogs have laid their eggs, and the toads are about to do so. Snails likewise are astir, waiting to nibble the young hawthorn leaves. At least two migrants have arrived, the chiff-chaff and the willow warbler (a country child's 'willow wren'). Whether lamblike or leonine, spring's resurgence resembles George Herbert's:

> Who would have thought my shrivel'd heart
> Could have recovered greenness? It was gone
> Quite underground.

At this season the greenness still is partly underground; not yet shall we see the beech leaf unfolding a haze on the hedges. Blackthorn, however, emits a cloud of white blossom which belies the name until you remember that the blackness belongs to the bark. Prunus, too, is flowering, and so are kingcups and those quivering anemones that justify their Greek name *anemos* or 'wind'.

Let no one suppose that these things are of interest only to townsfolk seeking to acquaint themselves with the common sights and sounds of the countryside. Innumerable suburban gardeners are admiring the crocus while listening to a blackbird. Let no one suppose that these things are of little interest to countryfolk who observe them every day. Innumerable villagers are admiring the Lent lilies while listening to a curlew. Computers and robots have not yet reduced everyone to the level of Wordsworth's 'Peter Bell':

> A primrose by a river's brim
> A yellow primrose was to him,
> And it was nothing more.

It is an old pastime, though still instructive, to cite chapter and verse for the vagaries of the British weather and climate. Thus, writing from Kent on 9 March 1766 Richard Hayes noted: 'Very pleasant sunny warm day.' Writing from Hampshire on 7 March 1786 Gilbert White noted: 'Snow drifted over hedges and gates.' Writing from Warwickshire on 15 March 1868 Gerard Manley Hopkins noted: 'Fine and summer-like.' Writing from Radnorshire on 1 March 1876 Francis Kilvert noted: 'Wild wind and rain and hail.' In 1771 Gilbert White assessed the effects of a cold and dry March: 'Wheat hardly to be seen and no sign of grass.' In 1779 Thomas Henry Baker assessed the effects of a mild and moist March: 'Season of great fertility; the crop one fourth above a medium.' Twenty years later, utterly dispirited by the March winds, Elizabeth Iremonger relinquished hope: 'I believe', she wrote, 'that all the hot days are deferred to the next century.' Another woman, Mrs Piozzi, spoke for the farming community: 'How little do you townsfolk know how prejudicial is the weather to our Country Farmers and Labourers. When the Gardener came yesterday, scratching his head, saying there would be no wall-fruit this year, I could hardly answer civilly; but I did say, "For God's sake think about the hay and corn, and hang the fine people and their wall-fruit" '. In those years a lean season not only raised the price of a labourer's food but also reduced his wages by making him temporarily redundant. His hunger was exacerbated by a lack of those creature comforts which to us seem absolute necessities, yet to him would have been luxuries: clean clothes; heating that permeated the whole house, not simply one corner of the kitchen; a hot bath, a dry bed, a rainproof roof.

Not without reason do we hanker for the moment when the clocks are put forward, granting a so-called 'extra' hour of daylight which could have been obtained simply by getting up earlier. We wish the month over and done with, so that we may mow the lawn and hear the cuckoo. Those things will follow soon enough. For the present, it is wise to accept March as a bitter-sweet lozenge, allowing it to linger on the palate.

An Old Penny

Penelope MacBarra is known affectionately as Mrs Penny. Despite her age (she has lately acquired a great-grandson) and her widowhood (the Brigadier served with the Indian army) and her arthritis (which affects the left arm) . . . despite those things she leads a life so active that her daughters are trying to persuade her to give-up grooming the venerable mare and to reduce the number of her honorary presidencies.

A countrywoman born and bred—acquainted with Simla, no stranger to the Andes—Mrs Penny relishes the quietude of her present modest home; but she does regret that the nearest large town has become a commercial hive. As she remarked to the Chairman of the County Council: 'The skep still contains a few pleasant nooks and crannies, but to look for them is like seeking the jam in a doughnut, and even when you've found the jam you can never escape from the din of cars and lorries and aircraft. Of course', she admitted, 'I quite understand that it's nowadays considered very immoral to wish to escape from the din. But then, you see, I happen to believe that a great deal of modern immorality is rather moral. And vice versa.' Last week Mrs Penny made one of her thrice-yearly visits to the town, chiefly in order to buy something for the great-grandson's second birthday. Having driven forty-three miles in ninety-two minutes, she parked her small car in a space belonging to the society over which she presides. She then walked slowly toward the main street, glancing at any shop which displayed goods that were not designed to disintegrate as quickly as the customers could afford to buy replacements. Serve-yourself shops she ignored. Deafened by traffic and jostled by crowds, she consoled herself in remembering that she would soon be home again, hearing the birds and the brook and the breeze; no longer a stranger in a sea of strangers, but known and knowing; pausing to talk with Tom the roadman, and waving when young Dulcie led the cows from Five Acres.

Having chosen a birthday gift, Mrs Penny sought the

quietness of the cathedral precincts, where a Canon's twin sisters kept a restaurant at which she said to the waitress: 'Tea and toast, my dear. And if the Misses Brown can spare a moment, say that Penny would love to see them.'

At three o'clock she visited the society, where she smoked a cigarette while discussing the best way to cope with colic in persons under two years of age. Afterwards, crossing Dean's Yard, she met the society's honorary secretary, who complained: 'This town gets noisier every day. Just look at the crowds. Where do they all come from? I can remember . . .'

'Yes', Mrs Penny interrupted, 'I, too, remember when we could hear ourselves speak, when we could cross the road without running, and when a poached egg cost less than we now pay for a box of matches. But those years are past and won't ever return, so we must either hurry up and die or hurry home and live. I propose to do the latter. In fact, I shall be home in two hours' time, thank God.'

It may have been her own colloquial Te Deum that caused Mrs Penny to follow the path to the cathedral. On the steps she halted, gazing up at craftsmanship that surged like a psalm *in excelsis*. She admits that her own theology is eclectic. As an infant she had been nursed by a Scottish Calvinist; as a girl she had attended the Church of England; as a young woman, exiled to India, she had studied the pantheism of Hinduism and the life-denying ordinances of Buddhism. By the time she was thirty she had decided that it was all guess-work, and that Anglicanism *cum grano* was the best guess for English folk. 'But', she murmured, 'if they're using that dreadful new Prayer Book I shan't stay to listen.'

They were not using it. Instead, as she knelt with the handful of worshippers, she heard cadences whose perfection was not amenable to improvement: 'Wherefore I pray and beseech you, as many as are here present, to accompany me with a pure heart and humble voice unto the throne of the heavenly grace, saying after me . . .' Mrs Penny duly whispered: 'Almighty and most merciful Father, we have erred and strayed from thy ways like lost sheep. We have followed too much the devices and desires of our own hearts . . . And there is no health in us. But thou, O Lord, have mercy upon us miserable offenders; spare thou them, O God, which confess their faults . . .'

At the very moment when Mrs Penny realized that she might not reach home before lighting-up time, the Prebend said: 'Lighten our darkness, we beseech thee, O Lord, and by thy great mercy defend us from all the perils and dangers of this night . . .' Making sure that the ignition key was still strapped to her wrist, Mrs Penny gathered up her handbag and parcels, tiptoed to the door, opened it gently, and stood once again on the steps, greeted by the drone of traffic, by Trade's tall temples looming like rectangular lighthouses, and by crowds that either hurried tensely or huddled sheepishly until a green lamp gave them permission to cross the street. In the garden of the deanery a blackbird sang, and from the cathedral's closed door came the chorus Nunc Dimittis.

The Bible had long ago taught Mrs Penny that the precepts of the market-place were old when Moses was young; but never before, she thought, had the precepts been so zealously practised by so many disciples. Descending the steps, she was soon engulfed among those precepts, which either ignored or derided the ethos of Evensong.

Assorted Company

Sometime ago a wise man coined a phrase: 'it takes all sorts to make a world.' It undoubtedly does, as I rediscovered while visiting several households in various parts of the country. The first of my hosts was not so much a householder as a caravan-occupier. Had he wished to do so, he could live comfortably in a sizeable house, but he prefers to lead a hermit's life on the edge of a wood. When I arrived, to learn whether he was still alive, he seemed reluctant to open the door. If he catches sight of someone in the lane he either turns back or hides behind a hedge. His letters and domestic supplies are left in a barn, to be collected after dark. Although normality is a vague and private condition, most people will regard the caravanner's seclusion as eccentric.

My next visit was to a household so gregarious that the caller seldom finds less than three other guests when he appears there. Grandparents wander in and out; babies crawl across the floor; cats crawl across the babies; the wife is talking nappies with another young mother; and the husband, a novelist, holds court in his study, chatting with the rector, the vet, the farmer on the hill, and a complete stranger who happened to pass while coffee was being served in the garden. When if at all, the novelist ever sleeps or earns his living I hardly know. It is not uncommon to see several cars parked outside the house at one o'clock on a winter morning. At seven o'clock on a summer morning I have arrived to find the milk girl and the roadman taking tea with a tramp in the kitchen.

There is, of course, a middle way between those two extremes, as followed by a widower who lives alone in a valley beside a trout stream. Still active and alert, he spends much time fishing, botanizing, birdwatching, and woodworking. Unlike the novelist, he may pass several days without speaking to anyone except the postman, but if you do find him at home, off goes the radio, out come the drinks, and you feel that he is genuinely pleased to see you. Moreover, he attends the parish council, the point-to-point, the vicarage fête, and the old folks' supper.

Not surprisingly, a house tends to reflect the householder, varying from spick and span to topsy-turvy. Few people allow their home to become dirty, but quite a number encourage it to remain untidy. By 'untidy' I do not mean the informality that is one of the pleasures of having small children and large dogs; I mean rather a mêlée in which the visitor finds a Hoover blocking the door, gumboots lying across the hall, and the kitchen cluttered with toys, dogs, cats, library books, shopping baskets, bedroom slippers, stray socks, laundered sheets, electric fires, a bundle of magazines (to be delivered to old Mr A) and a large parcel for Miss B (who was out when the van called). Despite their disorder, such families are often the most cordial of hosts, and will spend several moments battling through the bric-à-brac in order to make coffee or, as they put it, to 'find' some sherry. Other houses gleam so brilliantly that you feel you have reached an oriental shrine and must proceed barefoot. The dazzling decor suggests either that the wife spends her life 'going round' with a duster or that a girl from the village does so on her behalf. Nothing is out of place. The ornaments appear to have been manufactured adhesively *in situ*. Even the chair covers are partly protected by other covers. You certainly brush your posterior before sinking into a settee.

As with householders, so with households . . . appearances may deceive. You notice, for example, that the dormer windows of a Tudor cottage have been enlarged, and that the new owner has turned the thatched woodshed into a flat-roofed garage. Inside the cottage you find strip lighting in place of oil lamps, a gas stove on the blocked hearth, carpets over the flagstones, and furniture so aggressively up-to-date that in a few years' time it will seem old-fashioned. Entering another house, late Victorian at its worst, and thinking: 'No one could ever do anything with this place,' you discover that the owners have refuted you by an adroit application of white paint and by a correct arrangement of furniture which, since it was country-made, looks well in any country house. When you leave, and turn to glance at the unprepossessing exterior, you feel as though you are confronting someone whose sweet nature eclipses a lack of physical attraction.

Myself, I have a special fondness for houses which enjoy the best of both worlds, the receptive readiness and the relaxed retirement. One such is a manor in Northamptonshire. The cobbled yard is clean, the panelled hall glistens, the reception rooms remind you of people who are always neat but never conspicuous. However, if you glance through the so-called 'study' window you notice a hair-drier, the remains of lunch for two, several raincoats, three buckets, and a puppy chewing the rug. In short, the householders remain permanently at ease, knowing that a visitor can be received at any moment, and that when he or she has left, the host and hostess may, as we say, let their hair down, or at least rescue the rug. But appearances are not the whole of domesticity. Like its well-washed occupants, every house has a distinctive aroma. I am told that my own house smells of apples and bees-wax. Gerard Manley Hopkins was greeted by a similar fragrance at the farm in the Elwy Valley:

> Comforting smell breathed at very entering,
> Fetched fresh, as I suppose, from some sweet wood.

Bump in the Night

'Do you believe in ghosts?' Some people will answer 'Yes', as they did when I was staying at a fenland hotel that had reported strange nocturnal noises. Among the guests were a Cambridge don and several undergraduates who hoped to solve the mystery by keeping an all-night vigil. On learning this, one of the other guests proposed to create his own things that go bump in the night, but fair play prevailed, and the psychic researchers were left undisturbed by trickery.

As a sceptic in such matters, I went to sleep without feeling any qualms, and was not at all surprised when, next morning, the investigators reported that they had neither heard nor seen anything unusual. Some of them, no doubt, supposed that their arrival had coincided with a ghostly *nox non*.

Despite my scepticism, however, I admit that I have had two eerie experiences while walking with friends in Devon. The first occurred as we were wondering which of three paths to follow. Seeing a man higher up the lane, I said: 'He may know. I'll go and ask.' Before I could reach him, the man entered a field, but when I came to the place of entry I could find no gate or gap by which he might have passed through the thick and very tall hedge. Feeling foolish as well as mystified, I returned to my companions. The only explanation I could offer was: 'I still say I saw someone.' As we were all sceptics we dismissed the incident, though I confess that it continued to puzzle me.

At the end of our walk I saw a little girl, about fifty yards ahead, and as no house was visible I wondered where she was going. Then, like the man, the child entered a field; but once again I found no gap in the hedge. Not wishing to make a second exhibition of myself, I said to the friend alongside me: 'Did you see a little girl just now?' He replied: 'Yes. She went into that field.' Then he, too, found that not even a sturdy adult could have forced a way through. Now a walker may suffer one optical illusion, but when he suffers two within the hour, the second of which was shared by a reliable witness, he may indeed be tempted to doubt the validity of his own scepticism. The rest of my friends were certainly puzzled when they learned what had happened. From time to time we still discuss the incidents, but without ever being able to account for them.

On our way home I recalled the inconsistency of Thomas Huxley, who refused to join a number of eminent Victorians in studying psychic phenomena. The subject, he declared, was unworthy of a scientist's attention; yet he had already told Charles Kingsley: 'Sit down before the fact like a little child, follow humbly wherever and into whatever abyss nature leads you, or you shall learn nothing.'

Country houses are said to be a favourite haunt of ghosts. I remember reading about some strange events at the Yorkshire home of Major George Anne. During the 1940s he heard midnight shufflings and a muffled voice. On another occasion several doors were slammed open and shut. At about the same time the major's wife awoke to find a man standing beside the fireplace. His clothes, she said, were Victorian, but when he realized that he had been seen he vanished.

It is not difficult to understand why some people believe in ghosts. For example, a friend and I used to rent a cottage on the Essex marshes, a remote place, accessible only via a track. On a dark and misty night we had driven within half a mile of the cottage when a weird figure appeared, wearing what looked like a shroud, and wielding a staff. His white beard completed the effect of Katharine Tynan's verse:

At night what things will stalk abroad,
What veiled shapes, and eyes of dread;
What phantoms in a lonely road,
And visions of the dead.

Before we could investigate, the apparition vanished, and although we flashed a torch we found no trace of him. Discussing the incident at supper, I said: 'Ghosts don't exist. It's all a fantasy.' My friend agreed, but could not help adding: 'Even so, it makes you think.'

'So does laudanum,' I replied. 'And look what it did to Coleridge.'

Next morning we learned that a party of monks were staying in the district.

If, unlike Huxley, you adopt a scientific attitude toward these things, you may reasonably disbelieve that ghosts really do clank around in chains, carrying their own head. You may likewise disbelieve that murdered men haunt the scene of the crime; such goings-on would confront us with a philosophical nightmare. Nevertheless, you must admit that some people do imagine apparitions, and that their descriptions of them are sincere. Perhaps the most famous ghost was the one which, so they said, haunted the royal palace at Elsinore in Denmark. Was Hamlet justified when he said that heaven and earth contain more mysteries than Horatio's philosophy dreamed of?

The Bonnie Banks

On my way to the Scottish Highlands I spent the night in an hotel at Luss, overlooking Loch Lomond, where one of the guests—a Mancunian—said to me: 'I would like to live on an island.'

'You do live on an island,' I replied.

'But . . .'

'Britain *is* an island. In fact, it is hundreds of islands.'

'Yes,' the Mancunian conceded, 'I suppose it is.' He glanced from the window, in the direction of one of the small islands which rise from Loch Lomond like green oases. 'What I really mean is, I'd like to be aware of living on an island. After all, Lancashire . . .'

'Lancashire,' I pointed out, 'does have an island.'

'Oh?'

'Pie Island. It lies off the Furness peninsula.'

'Is it inhabited?'

'Certainly. It has an hotel, or did have when I tried to land there. Unfortunately, the only transport was the postman's punt, and I arrived too late to get across. However, I did manage to visit one of the Loch Lomond islands. In fact, I was on it this morning.'

'How interesting. Do tell me about it.'

Pausing while a waiter refilled our coffee cups, I explained that I had met a farmer who lived within a few yards of the water. Perceiving my fondness for Scotland, he invited me to visit an island on which he pastured some of his sheep. Ten minutes later we boarded a small boat whose outboard engine was worked by a taciturn Highlander. The loch being calm, we soon reached the island, a few acres of grassland with some trees and a chalet. Seeing the sheep, I said: 'Cheviots.'

'Aye,' the farmer nodded. 'In the mountains we need a hardy breed.'

While the two men inspected the flock, I remarked that the setting was idyllic, dominated by mountains, lapped by water, warmed by sunlight.

'It's all right in this weather,' my host agreed, 'but not so long ago a man who was living alone in that chalet developed appendicitis. At midnight, with a blizzard raging, he lit a warning fire because he was too weak to row ashore, but the snow blotted out the island. Next day, when he failed to arrive at the usual time, someone rowed across and found him lying unconscious. They rang the hospital, of course, but all the roads were blocked, and before the ambulance arrived the poor fellow died of peritonitis.'

Following that sombre story, the taciturn Highlander said to the farmer: 'Has the Englishman seen all he wants?' I nodded, and we returned to the mainland.

In summer the banks of Loch Lomond cease to be bonnie. They are littered with beer cans, cigarette ends, newspapers, and the ashes of camp-fires. The road north to Crianlarich is a steep and sinuous crocodile of cars, and the loch itself carries an armada whose noise and numbers have increased since Keats complained that 'The Steam-boats on Loch Lomond take from the pleasure . . .' When Keats's contemporary, Rev. Thomas Dibdin, scaled Ben Lomond he found that not every prospect pleased him: 'Beneath our feet, the loch, with the steamers reduced to a cockle-shell, yet although at a height of 3,124 feet, we heard the noise of the steam escaping from the valves!'

Arriving in spring, I was more fortunate than the summer visitors. When a white yacht glided into the sunset, I shared Keats's happier impression of the loch: 'The evening was beautiful . . . nothing could surpass our fortune in the weather.' Nevertheless, the ascent of Ben Lomond requires sturdy limbs and strong boots. In 1882 Mary Howitt 'found the ascent from Rowardeman a laborious task of four hours . . . The bogs which intercepted our course every few yards required a good deal of boldness, contrivance, and circumspection to pass . . .'

The loch contains about thirty islands, one of which, Inversnaid, has the remains of a castle built by the Earls of Lennox. In Dr Johnson's day the castle served as a prison for lunatics and alcoholics. On another island Wordsworth met the lass who inspired one of his poems:

> Sweet Highland Girl, a very shower
> Of beauty is thy earthly dower . . .
> Thou wearest upon thy forehead clear
> The freshness of a mountaineer. . .

In a note to his poem about another of the islands, Wordsworth stated: 'On a small island, not far from the head of Loch Lomond, are some remains of an ancient building, which was for several years the abode of a solitary Individual, one of the last survivors of the Macfarlanes, once powerful in the district . . . this person then living there had acquired the appellation of "The Brownie". . .'

Loch Lomond is one of several places which regard themselves as a gateway to the Highlands. At Luss, for example, the mountains rise up, the land becomes wild, and the voice of Scottish nationalism is heard (Did not the taciturn Highlander refer to me as 'The Englishman'?). The road southward from Luss soon widens into a race track, the Highlands fall astern, the outskirts of Balloch appear, and Glasgow not far behind them. In the days of Sir Walter Scott's Rob Roy the road northward from Glasgow became wild while still within sight of the city: 'The road we had travelled,' Scott wrote, 'had become wild and open as soon as we had left Glasgow a mile or two behind, and was growing more dreary as we advanced. Huge continuous heaths spread before, behind, and around us in hopeless barrenness . . .' At Luss today a southbound traveller soon encounters an industrial wilderness wherein he feels as Robert Burns felt:

> My heart's in the Highlands, my heart is not here;
> My heart's in the Highlands, a-chasing the deer . . .

4

A Long Day's March

Spring is the best season for walking. Summer may become too hot, autumn too wet, winter too dark; but when the March days have lengthened and the April showers abate, a countryman likes to stretch his legs as far as they will comfortably go. Wordsworth could walk from Grasmere to Penrith and back in one day, a journey of forty mountainous miles. Even half that distance will seem hard-going to sedentary persons, yet in April a hale and habitual walker can easily cover twenty miles between dawn and dusk. The chief requisites are reasonably dry weather and a firm conviction that speed is neither necessary nor desirable.

Yesterday a friend of mine did walk twenty miles, and today he tells me that he feels all the better for it. Since I joined him for much of the way, our procedure may interest anyone who wishes to achieve a similar sense of well-being. Starting at 8.30 a.m., we walked for two hours at three-and-a-half miles an hour, resting for five minutes at the end of the first lap and for thirty minutes at the seventh mile. Between about 11 a.m. and 1.30 p.m. we covered the same distance at the same pace, so that more than half the journey was accomplished before we halted for coffee and sandwiches in a wayside barn.

Continuing refreshed at 2 p.m., we covered only a couple of miles during the next two hours, not because we felt weary but because we visited a church, telephoned an acquaintance, and spent some time talking with a man whose mother had worked at a Lincolnshire woad factory. 'How interesting,' my friend

told him. 'I'd always imagined that woad went out with Queen Boudicca.' At that point we parted company; I to spend the night with friends, he to continue his journey until four o'clock, when he noticed a derelict horse rake in an overgrown field. As you may know, Edwardian horse rakes have a sprung seat, so there he sat with his back against a drystone wall, taking the last of the coffee and then the penultimate sandwich (the final one, he told me, went to a robin that had sung for his supper). When a shower of rain descended, he sheltered behind the wall.

With scarcely four miles to go, and more than enough daylight in which to cover them, he remembered George Borrow's boast that, having walked fifteen miles, he could finish the next five in an hour; but my friend remembered also the Dickens character who died of spontaneous combustion. The last lap, therefore, was taken leisurely, yet not too leisurely, because path-finding after dark should be attempted only by those who, like Scott's wayfarer, can say;

> As safe to me the mountain way
> At midnight as in blaze of day.

By this time my friend confessed that he began to feel tired, though not unpleasantly so; on the contrary, the sensation was akin to the drowsiness of a healthy person when bedtime approaches at the end of a hard day's work, mental or physical. Some activities will tire the limbs more rapidly than walking does. They demand a greater co-ordination of mind and body, and for that reason they narrow the mental processes. Even a horseman must concentrate on keeping his seat. A walker, by contrast, moves almost as spontaneously as he breathes, so that his brain can range widely, at one moment admiring the view, at another moment pondering such matters as immortality, bird migration, the price of petrol, Hartley's epistemology, and the respective merits of roast chicken and lamb chops.

Sedentary people may retort that many non-exercisers reach a hale old age; that many over-exercisers never reach old age at all; and that Carlyle walked the fifty-four miles from Muirkirk to Dumfries in one day, yet was subject to dyspeptic melancholia. All of those statements are true, and none of them can refute a fourth truth, namely, that a long walk is sometimes more efficacious than a bottle of medicine. The walk itself, however, ought not to be taken as Timothy took wine, solely for his stomach's sake. The mind must be jogged as well as the body. Mere foot-slogging causes exhaustion which in turn deadens the brain. Unlike a motorist, the walker ought not to spend his time staring at the road ahead. He should stare rather at the hills, valleys, trees, brooks, birds, and such buildings as are worthy of attention. He should observe the ways in which geology has conditioned the landscape, its crops, its crafts, its industries, its architecture. He should note further the ways in which the Celts, Romans, Saxons, Normans, and later generations of Britons have transformed—not invariably for the better—an island of dense forest and extensive swamps. Above all, the walker must avoid a painful introspection. Heaven help the man who is alone in a wood with his worries.

Clothes being a matter of taste, one hesitates to prescribe an appropriate walking costume. Myself, I prefer plus-fours (they are nowadays abbreviated as plus-twos). Such garments help to keep the legs dry and to protect them against nettles and briars. Since walking is, for me an everyday event, I would not willingly imitate the hikers whose costumes suggest that they are bound for Mont Blanc.

Food and drink should be carried during a long trek, but refrain from munching while you walk, for that will rob you of part of your reward, which is hunger and the prospect of satisfying it. If you reach journey's end after seven o'clock you will need a substantial meal, the last of the day. If you arrive before six o'clock you will be wise to take a lighter meal and to supplement it before retiring, which is my friend's custom after a long day's march. And so it came to pass that at six o'clock, in the comfort of a farmhouse kitchen, he consumed two boiled eggs, four slices of toast, a hunk of cake, and several cups of tea. Three hours later he partook of a snack, and soon after that, while brushing his teeth, he nearly fell asleep.

England's Day

While visiting a primary school fête the other day I mingled with a generation that will probably never even hear of names which are woven into the fabric of English history . . . names like Rutland and Westmorland and Huntingdonshire. The statutory destruction of those ancient counties was applauded by people who regard regional pride as an archaic emotion, at all times subordinate to the whims of Messrs Industry and Commerce.

Admittedly, regional pride does sometimes overstep the limit, as, for instance, when a Westmorlander declares: 'There's nobbut twa counties in't North, and the second of 'em is Cumberland.' By crossing the Eamont Bridge, from what used to be Westmorland into what used to be Cumberland, you may hear a comparable declaration, but with the precedence reversed. If you question the Westmorlander you will probably find that he is not utterly blind to the merits of other counties. 'I was born and bred in Westmorland', he will say, 'and I hope to end my days here. But . . .' then follows the qualification: 'I admit that Cumberland contains higher mountains and more lakes. I admit that the Border Regiment was garrisoned in Cumberland. I'll even admit I visit Penrith in order to buy Cumberland sausage, but I still say Westmorland is better.' At that point you would do well to let the matter drop, because any attempt to define the word 'better' will elicit little more than: 'Well I just mean *better*.'

There is an amusing clash of regional pride in R.D. Blackmore's *Lorna Doone*, whose plot moves between Devon and Somerset, at places where both counties include a part of Exmoor. Since the Blackmores were a North Devon family, and since it was from his grandfather, a North Devon parson, that Blackmore first learned the legend of the Doones, he was accused of giving undue prominence to Devon, a charge which he denied: 'Nowhere', he wrote, 'have I said, or even implied, that Exmoor lies mainly in Devonshire . . .' Moreover, the book's hero, Jan Ridd, stated his own position clearly: 'I try to speak impartially, belonging no more to Somerset than I do to Devon, living upon the borders and born of either county.' As though to reduce the rivalry by multiplying the rivals, Blackmore introduced a Cornish girl, Gwenny Carfax, who roundly told the Exmoor folk that a single Cornishman is 'better than any two men to be found in Devon, or any four in Somerset'. This attempt to keep the peace insulted Somerset twice as much as it displeased Devon.

No other part of Britain has a tradition of county pride comparable with the English, for when England was already a united kingdom, the rest of the region—Scotland, Ireland, Wales—were still fighting among themselves. Not needing to unite against a dominant neighbour, mediaeval England was able to foster those regional identities which almost supplanted a national identity, causing the English to become less nationalist than their fellow-Britons. Saints David and Andrew and Patrick still arouse fervour, but St. George's Day passes unnoticed by the majority of English folk, who are now so accustomed to yielding to non-English influences that they would feel themselves guilty of an offence if on St George's Day they unfurled their national flag. Many are unaware that they possess such a flag.

English folk who admire the unique cultures and traditions of Scotland and Ulster and Wales find it strange that while some Britons parade with anti-English placards (and occasionally with bombs), the English would be reviled as racists if they carried banners bearing such devices as 'Scots, Go Home' and 'Too Many Taffys in Taunton'. Whether one resents the fact or not, England has for centuries been the senior partner in numbers, in arms, in commerce, in industry, and in the arts. Without England—which is to say, without the English tax-payers—the rest of the kingdom would soon look and feel very lean; yet the mass of Englishmen either do not know or have ceased to value their forebears' achievement. Were Milton living at this hour, he would need to repeat his famous exhortation: 'Lords and Commons of England, consider what nation it is whereof ye are.' But if he continued to style himself 'John Milton, Englishman,' the Racist Board might warn him that it really was time to drop the word 'England'.

Certainly our regional prides were often arrogant; no less certainly they have mellowed. The Men of Kent may affect to look down on the Kentish Men, and the Red Rose and the White may dispute the prowess of Paynter and Botham, but at close of play both sides will sink their pride in a pint of beer. Unfortunately, regional pride is nowadays tainted by a commercial allegiance which allows someone from another county, or even from a distant land, to play cricket for Barsetshire and then, at a higher wage, for Darsetshire, though the stranger had never entered either of those countries until the club managers invited him to name his price. True patriotism, by contrast, rests on love, which itself springs from old acquaintance. Having stated his own case, a patriot expects other counties and other countries to do the same and thereafter to dwell in amity with all. That kind of pride still flourishes among countryfolk who, although they may have visited the Alps, feel no wish to forsake the Chilterns, or the

Cotswolds, or the Cheviots. Walter de la Mare expressed that lifelong love in a poem called 'England':

> No lovelier hills than thine have laid
> My tired thoughts to rest:
> No peace of lovelier valleys made
> Like peace within my breast.
>
> My heart within me faints to roam
> In thought even far from thee;
> Thine be the grave whereto I come,
> And thine my darkness be.

Something to Read

While watching the sunset and hearing the rooks, Mr Chips suddenly shivered. April or not, it was time to go indoors. He therefore walked away from the lake, up the terraced gardens and thence to his quarters above the stables at the hall. As he climbed the staircase he heard the gardener's wife calling from the courtyard: 'It's a bit nippy this evening, Sir, so I've lit the fire for you.' Mr Chips turned, sneezed, and replied: 'Bless you.'

Deprived of a housekeeper when his widowed sister married Sir Richard, the retired schoolmaster had gladly accepted his new brother-in-law's invitation to reside at the hall, in three snug rooms with a balcony. Sir Richard capped his generous gesture by modifying the stable clock, which now strikes the hour only, and cannot be heard a mile away.

Entering his book-lined study, Mr Chips was greeted by a scene that prompted him to read about it while he was looking at it. 'Hugh Walpole', he murmured, reaching for a book, from which he read aloud: 'You find your way by the light of the fire to the lamp, light it, and then turn. Your books crowd in upon you, they are pressing, urgent . . .' At that moment the telephone rang, inviting him to join some unexpected guests at the rectory. He hesitated, glanced at the books, and said: 'Not tonight. Thank you, all the same. There are some books I wish to look at. The what? No, nothing special . . . just some books.'

Having thrown another log on the fire, he lit a pipe and then ran his hand along the shelves, choosing Gilbert White, whom he began to read, still standing at the shelf. After a few sentences, however, he replaced *Selborne.* It was not quite what he needed. Next he tried Sir Thomas Browne, savouring the style while remembering the sunset: 'Thus there are two Books whence I collect my Divinity; besides that written one of God, another of his servant Nature, that universal and publick Manuscript, that lies expansed unto the Eyes of all: those that never saw him in the one, have discover'd Him in the other.' Usually an equable and decisive person, Mr Chips felt both puzzled and displeased when even Browne failed to fit his mood. Herrick sounded too light, Milton looked too heavy. For some moments Robert Bridges prevailed, but he, too, was set aside. 'Poetry', Mr Chips decided, 'is wine. I need prose . . . a glass of ale.'

More than ever piqued by his untypical dalliance, he drew aside the curtain and looked down on the lake, which was already speckled with stars. The glow had faded from the west, the wind had dropped, the daffodils bowed their penitential heads, and one thrush sang one last song, partly as good night to the day, partly as good evening to the night. Despite the keen air, Mr Chips knew that the spring had arrived and was revealing itself more clearly every day. Lowering the curtain, he returned to his books.

If it was prose he sought, why not try *A Discourse on Method*? Or should he choose—when did he buy it and why?—*The Wine Trade with Gascony: 1300-1450*? From the shelf nearest a photograph of the Leander crew in 1930 he sampled and swiftly rejected *Relativity for Laymen*, together with Carlyle's *Life of John Sterling* and *Keynes: a Summary.* Macaulay, then, or Froude? No; history seemed too long for an hour by the fire.

Seeking guidance in his search, he re-opened Hugh Walpole's essay: 'As you stand by one of the bookcases there is a glorious instant of indecision . . .' Mr Chips closed the book. 'Instant of indecision?' he muttered. 'My own indecision has been going on for nearly ten minutes.' With mounting frustration he passed over Plautus, Pater, Elia, Evoe, and a prose translation of *The Cid.* Likewise he declined *Allenby in Palestine* and *Austin Seven Handbook 1925*. However, one name did cause him to blink. 'Kafka? Who on earth gave me that fellow? I'm damned certain I never got beyond chapter three. Kafka was a case history. That's why the loonies love him. Ah, this is more like it . . . *In Defence of Pink.* What a splendid title.' But again he was wrong; Robert Lynd proved too fragile. De Quincey, in the present mood, sounded rotund, and Matthew Arnold too didactic. By way of respite from his dilemma Mr Chips went onto the balcony, looking and listening. A vixen barked, and after than an owl hooted, very shrill. Ducks on the lake gaggled awhile; then the silence returned, lit as it were, by tubs of daffodils gleaming on the cobbled yard below, 'All right', Mr Chips resolved, 'it'll have to be a lucky dip.' Re-entering the study, he stretched out his arm and took the first book that came to hand. Without glancing at the title, he pulled his chair toward the fire, relit his pipe, and then examined the book. 'Good Lord', he exclaimed, 'why ever didn't I think of it before?' He stirred the logs, wriggled the chair closer to the fire, and settled down to read. Three minutes later he began to smile, then he chuckled, then he laughed. Still laughing, he rose to answer the telephone. It was his sister, reminding him of the Major's funeral tomorrow. 'It isn't', she added, 'a laughing matter.'

'I know it isn't', Mr Chips agreed.

'Then why laugh, my dear?'

'I wasn't laughing.'

'But you were. I heard you.'

'What I mean is, I wasn't laughing at the funeral. I was merely . . . well, as a matter of fact, I'm in the middle of Bardell v. Pickwick.'

A Kind of Food

'Colour', said Richard Jefferies, 'is a kind of food . . . a drop of wine for the spirit.' There is certainly much colour to be seen during May; not, of course, so various as June's, nor so flamboyant as October's, yet fresher than in August and profuser than in April.

Some people relish most the month's diversity of colour, from the last daffodil to the first lilac, and between those two a rainbow of wall-flowers, primrose, pansy, bluebell, forget-me-not, campion, sweet-william, apple-blossom, and sometimes a rosebud alongside an Antirrhinum. Other people set greater store by a single colour, green, which, having been announced in April, now enters and is seen by all. It is fitting that an English countryman's unofficial national anthem should be called 'Greensleeves'.

The view from this garden is predominantly green. In fact, no other colours catch the eye, unless you include a blue sky and the white sheep. The land beyond the garden falls away steeply into a climb, thereafter climbing to a wide and lofty horizon. Most of that land is pasturage; but parts of the higher ground are wooded, and in one place the trees rise from the banks of a stream flowing through the combe, too deep-set to be visible.

Although nearly everything is green, the shades of greenness are so numerous, and the differences between some of them so slight, that only a botanist could detect and classify them. Of course, any countryman will identify the conifer plantation on the left of the summit; its greenery is very dark, like that of certain army vehicles. Any countryman will identify the plantation in the centre of the summit, which some people might describe as coniferous, though its trees are larches and therefore deciduous. During April, when the reddish buds unfolded it seemed that nothing could outshine those larches; but in May they are outshone by a patch of beech nearby.

Looking down at a holly tree in the lower paddock, and then up at the hilltop conifers, it is difficult to decide which of them is the greener; the holly, perhaps. An oak tree, by contrast, looks quite pale until it is viewed against beeches, and then it looks quite yellow. Aspens, however, appear rather grey, at any rate when a breeze stirs their leaves. Only one lime is visible, and only one pine (at the far end of the drive); yet how markedly the colours differ from each other. Compared with the pine, the lime seems almost as pale as the beech, whereas the difference between the lime and the ash is slight when the two are seen in the shade.

If you cross a couple of fields, taking care not to slither down the steepest part of the second, you reach a stream and several white willows. Like aspens, a willow appears to lose some of its greenness when the wind upturns the foliage. Many reeds and rushes grow beside the stream, each variety wearing its own shade of green. This diverse spectrum is not confined to tall plants. The banks of the stream are bright with thistles, dandelions, daisies, docks, bracken, primroses, bee-orchis; and there also the leaves and stems of each kind differ from the rest, even as the colour of ivy differs from the withered daffodils, and they from the withered snowdrops. The greenness of a single plant may reveal variations on itself, for the lower leaves on a rose bush are sometimes darker than those on a young shoot.

Likewise the beech coverts vary, especially those on the foothills of the moor, where the lower and south-facing trees are already in full leaf while the upper and north-facing trees bear buds that have not yet unfolded. Higher still, at 800 feet, parts of the ash hedges remain leafless. At 1,000 feet, where only a thorn can thrive, the wind-worn branches seem almost as bare as in December. At 1,700 feet the few thorns that do exist are bent parallel with the ground. Not one is more than six feet high. All must wait until late May before their leaves unfold.

Although none of the smaller farms hereabouts grow trees for a wide commercial market, the woods are by no means unprofitable. Quite apart from their role as purifiers of the air, some of them are felled as fuel for the farmers' use, and others go in small quantities to builders and carpenters. One man fells his alders to serve as stakes in the garden. Small branches from other trees—known locally as 'sticks'—he gives to his friends.

Cricket bats are not the only things that require good willow. At a cottage on the road between Battle and Hailsham in Sussex I used to visit a brother and sister who made trugs. The brother once took me to a stream on a neighbouring farm, where he and the owner did business. The trug-maker soon found the willows best-suited to his needs. In less than six minutes he had chosen and marked what he wanted, and a couple of minutes later a price was agreed. Other crafts require other timber. Sycamore, for example, polishes easily as a piece of furniture, especially if it is figured. Walnut is nowadays so valuable that dealers pay cash on the spot. Sweet-chestnut is used as fencing. Black poplar serves the few clog-makers still in business. Spruce, which carpenters call white deal, makes a ship's mast. Douglas fir may become a railway sleeper. Larch goes underground as a pit prop, and into the air as a telephone pole. White mulberry feeds silk-worms. And in May they all wear their finest green livery.

At Home

I went out to hear the dawn chorus the other morning, and what a morning it was, blue-skied and full of promises which, said the weather forecast, would be fulfilled. Just such a scene must have evoked Laurie Lee's spring song:

> If ever I saw blessing in the air,
> I see it now in this still early day,
> Where lemon-green the vaporous morning drips
> Wet sunlight on the powder of my eyes.

In the wood beside the garden the beech leaves were almost translucent. Under them a few pink campions dappled the bluebells that shone like a tarn in the sun. The birds sang full-throated, led by a thrush on the topmost branch of a sycamore.

From somewhere in the back row of that chorus a cuckoo tried to impose his own tempo on the singers. When an owl joined in, not ten yards from where I stood, the shriek sounded strange, so early in the day.

After breakfast I sauntered downhill through the wood to a high-banked lane which is very steep, very narrow, very unfrequented. Peering from the wood onto the lane, I saw the heads of three walkers who were telling one another what an enjoyable holiday they were having. Strangers being rare in these parts, I was about to greet them *de haut en bas*, but they must have heard my footsteps, because one of the trio glanced up, looking rather startled. 'Does the lane', he called, 'get any steeper?'

'The lane', I replied, 'hasn't yet started to get steep.'

'Oh.' The stranger stared at the bend which half-concealed a 1-in-3 gradient. 'Yes,' he agreed. 'I see what you mean. Do *you* climb it often?'

'Not often. Just once a day.'

'Oh. By the way, does it lead anywhere?'

'I think the best answer is No. But if you continue until you reach a crossroads, and then turn left, and then right, and then left, and then again left, and finally right . . . if you do all those things you'll eventually reach a village.'

'With a pub?'

'I'm afraid not.'

'Any shops?'

'One.'

'Oh. Still, it's all very beautiful.'

Then the walkers plodded on, out of sight, out of hearing; but I remained in the wood peering down at the lane, which was lined with bluebells, campions, primroses, and here and there an Orchis. As though sharing the walkers' mood, I said to myself: 'Where would I like to be, on this bright May morning?' By way of answer I remembered the Crook of Lune, under the lee of the Westmorland fells, where a stone bridge spans a river whose murmurous water deepens the stillness. I remembered also the lane that climbs from Boscastle in Cornwall, crossing little streams, entering hilltop woods, and coming at last to St

Juliot, a parish without a village, where Thomas Hardy met his first wife, the rector's sister-in-law; a meeting which inspired his novel, *A Pair of Blue Eyes*, and—decades later—a sequence of nostalgic poems.

Returning to the garden, I thought of another steep lane, the one from Lingen in Herefordshire to Presteigne in Radnorshire (it used to have a signboard, 'Cyclists are advised to dismount'). From the summit of that lane you overlook a large tract of England and Wales, with woods dominating the Welsh side, and Hay Bluff jutting out like the paw of an enormous lion. Taking care not to trample the bluebells, I thought how pleasant it would be to revisit the bluebells in the woods above Bix Bottom, following a track through the Oxfordshire Chilterns; and after that I remembered a lane on the Isle of Skye, where two peat-diggers had waved as I passed, like ships in mid-ocean.

Stepping over the dry-stone wall and into the garden again, I took to a deck-chair, remembering Little Bedwyn and its thatched cottages beside a Wiltshire canal within sight of Savernake Forest; there, too, the bluebells outshine the water. But would it not be even more pleasant to reach the Silent Valley, a green oasis at the foot of the Mourne Mountains in Ulster, with views of the sea and the red-sail fishing boats? By this time my plans for a holiday had become a litany of impossibilities because, while wishing to be in the vicar's garden on Holy Island, I wished at the same moment to stride across the Downs from Firle Beacon to Seaford in Sussex, and to drive leisurely along those twenty unoccupied miles between Newcastleton and Hawick in Roxburghshire. Then a gull soared overhead, so high that he could sight both the Atlantic and the Severn Sea, which led me to think of Holderness, a coastal corner of Yorkshire, where lanes lead to farms that have gone the way of Lyonesse.

While I was remembering the grass-covered Roman road near Caio in old Carmarthenshire, my deck-chair travels were interrupted by a woodpecker drumming a tattoo. Peering through the trees, I could see a skyline of hills. Turning round, I saw another hilly skyline, and knew that beyond it lay an even loftier arc which in a few weeks' time would glow with purple heather. It was then that I answered my own question, swiftly and decisively. 'On this bright May morning', I said, 'I would like to be where I am.'

5

People and Places

Are we ever wholly content with our environment? Does a hill farmer never envy the lowlander whose house is sheltered from the wind? Does a lowlander never envy the hill farmer whose house commands a view of the mountains? Do Sutherland crofters never envy Cornwall's sunshine? Do Surrey commuters never envy Shropshire's car-free by-lanes? Desirable though our residence may be, surely it reveals a flaw, a less than perfect feature, a lack of this, an excess of that?

While wandering through Gloucestershire I could not help comparing the beauty of its Cotswold villages with the plain-faced architecture of North Devon, for Exmoor and the foothills possess nothing that can be set alongside Broadway, Bibury, or the Slaughters. E. V. Lucas was right when he said of the Cotswolds: 'The humblest barn is more beautifully ecclesiastic than the most pretentious of our latter-day churches.' Turning south from Gloucestershire to Oxfordshire and Berkshire, I noticed that there also the best of the villages—Yattendon, Ewelme, Great Tew—far excelled any in my own part of the world. A few days later, while driving through Sussex and Kent, I thought how pleasant it would be to live at Goudhurst or Shipley or Poynings. Heading homeward via Hampshire, I continued to notice the difference between the villages there and those in North Devon, which have no answer at all to Selborne and the offbeat hamlets that were Edward Thomas's happy hunting ground above Petersfield.

This disparity can be partly explained in terms of geology.

Regions that were densely wooded—Cheshire, for example—contain many magpie or timbered houses, whereas relatively treeless regions—North Cornwall is one—contain houses built of local stone. Even when timber was easily available, several regions—Lakeland and the Cotswolds among them—preferred to use their own stone. Variations on the same theme occur throughout the Chilterns and along the Norfolk coast,

where the builders were able to give the houses a facing of local flints. Similarly the Quantocks in Somerset contain many houses that were built of local sandstone. By affecting their income, geology affected people's ability to discriminate. Thus, the limestone belt between Wiltshire and Northamptonshire yielded fertile pastures which in turn enabled squires and yeomen to employ the best masons and the best materials. In mountainous or moorland places, however, the inhabitants grubbed a meagre living from a poor soil, and lacked both the means and the taste which elsewhere created the houses at Lavenham, Ledbury, Lingfield, Child's Wickham, Sutton Courtenay, Tredington, and Bledlow.

Meanwhile, as I came within fifty miles of home, the traffic had dwindled so sharply that the roads in West Somerset were comparatively quiet. A fact which went a long way toward compensating for the less impressive architecture.

I yield to no one in my admiration of the Weald, the Chilterns, the Downs, Cliveden Reach, Epping Forest, the Essex marshes. Nevertheless, all those places are either encircled or penetrated by lorries and cars, and the inhabitants regard London as their regional capital.

As though to prove the point, on the road from Honiton to Tiverton I met only three vehicles in a dozen miles. Beyond Tiverton, on the old road to South Molton, nearly eighteen miles without entering a village, I saw only six vehicles, two of which were tractors parked beside a gate. From South Molton, an attractive little market town, I drove six miles through steep and twisting lanes, passing only a few farmhouses; and so home to a companionable seclusion which I would not exchange for the traffic at Broadway or Petworth or Amersham. My homecoming, of course, was not one man's monopoly. Something like it is shared by Northumbrians who, having left the Newcastle road, delve into the depths of the Cheviots at Ingham. It is shared by Cornish folk who, having left the Bodmin race-track, follow wooded lanes to St Breward. It is shared by Lincolnshire folk who, having left the Skegness road, climb leisurely to Somersby on the Wolds. It is shared also by Herefordshire folk who, having left the lorry-laden Shrewsbury road, come at last to the quietude of Lingen; by Buckinghamshire folk when they leave the main Aylesbury road and climb the lane to Little Hampden; by Scottish lowlanders when they leave the main Glasgow road and come at last to Leadhills; by Durham folk when they leave the industrial zones and cross the moors to Middleton-in-Teesdale; by Welsh folk when they reach the hills above St Davids; by Dorset folk when they leave the holiday route to Cornwall and enter the peace of Winterbourne Came.

Architecture is only a feature of an environment. A friend of mine inherited a splendid seventeenth-century house in Lakeland, but during the best months of the year the cars and crowds are so dense that he seeks refuge on the Essex marshes. I have visited houses which are either ugly or uninteresting, yet all of them stand in deep country, and one of them can be approached only via a track across several fields. The occupants of those houses are not misanthropic. They entertain, and are entertained by, friends living in the district. Ultimately, of course, it is a matter of temperament. Some people enjoy noise and crowds; others do not. The latter must sometimes accept the fact that the shops are too far away, that the climate is less than kindly, and that the house itself is ill-designed. Such people need to count each boon weighing it against the banes from which they have escaped.

The Merriest Month

It seems appropriate that the names of the two fairest months are the names of women also—May and June. To ask whether the one excels the other is akin to asking whether rice excels sago. The answer will vary with the assessor's taste. May is wholly of the spring, whereas June is partly of the summer. The former is the fresher, the latter is the riper. Sir William Watson preferred the former,

> What is so sweet and dear
> As a prosperous morn in May,
> The valiant prime of the day,
> And the dauntless youth of the year . . .

May was long ago dubbed the merry month, but 'merry' has lost its original quality, which meant something agreeable, soothing, heartening. Edmund Spenser, for example, looked back with gratitude to his education at Merchant Taylors' in 'mery London, my most kyndly Nurse'. Another poet wished to 'Extole the merrie month of May'. Composers, too, have celebrated May. King Henry VIII's song book, which contains thirty-four of his own pieces, observes how pleasant it is

In May, that lusty season,
To gather the flowers down
By the meadows green . . .

The spelling of the next two lines evokes a century less sophisticated than our own:

The byrdys sang on every syde
So meryly, it joyed my hart.

During the seventeenth century the village maypole was so popular that the Stuarts defended it against the spoil-sport Puritans. This defence took the form of a royal proclamation, commonly called *The King's Book of Sports*, which was issued by James I in 1618 and re-issued by Charles I in 1633. 'Our good people', it decreed, 'be not disturbed, letted, nor discouraged from . . . having of May games, and setting up of Maypoles . . . so as the same be had in due and convenient time without impediment or neglect of Divine Service . . .' Cromwell and the Puritan non-conformists ordered *The King's Book of Sports* to be 'burned by the hand of the common hangman in Cheapside and other usual places . . .'. Any Londoners who possessed a copy of the book were required to bring it to be burned at noon on 10 May 1643. The same dissenters abolished both Christmas and maypoles. 'No Maypole', they said, 'shall hereafter be set up . . .' If any village disobeyed the ban, the parish constable was fined every week until the totem had been removed.

As one would expect, the poets looked more graciously on spring. Milton was not the only townsman who has turned countryward at lilac time:

As one who long in populous City pent,
Forth issuing on a Summers Morn to breathe
Among the pleasant Villages and Farmes
The smell of Grain, or tedded Grass, or Kine . . .

Another townsman, Keats, borrowed Milton's self-description:

> To one who has been long in city pent
> 'Tis very sweet to look into the fair
> And open face of heaven . . .

The sight and scent of hawthorn blossom, or of a wood paved with bluebells, are indeed beautiful. On a bright May morning even the pessimists saunter in the sun, sharing Thomas Hardy's mood:

> This is the weather the cuckoo likes,
> And so do I.

The rest of the poem is still up-to-date, not least when it remarks that in May the villagers drink their ale on a bench outside The Travellers Rest:

> And maids come forth, sprig-muslin drest,
> And citizens think of the south and west,
> And so do I.

In the south and west the sweet of the year arrives earlier than elsewhere. Cornwall's daffodils bloom before Yorkshire's; Dorset's primroses fade before Durham's. There is some truth in the saying that spring travels northward at a speed of one hundred miles a week. Nevertheless, comparable variations can be found within a relatively small area, as in North Devon, where the wall-flowers at Barnstaple bloom in early February, scarcely a dozen miles from the Exmoor foothills, where some of the wall-flowers do not bloom until late April. Similarly, the leaves on a hedge halfway down a mountainous lane may unfold several days before the leaves on the same hedge two hundred yards higher up. Altitude and soil combine with aspect and genetics to ensure that an oak comes into leaf while another oak—of the same age, standing less than ten yards away—is still leafless.

These familiar sights and sounds never cloy, but with each annual re-appearance seem new. In springtime you will find a man strolling hand-in-hand with his small grandson, each halting to hear a blackbird or to pick a flower or to watch a lamb. The man may have greeted those things seventy times; the child may be greeting them for the first time; yet the wonderment of age is at least as deep as the wonderment of youth, and may indeed be deeper because it has perceived the shallowness of its own understanding.

A Pleasant Surprise

Not long ago I went to visit my old Chiltern friend, hoping to find him in good health, but by no means certain that he was still alive. Under a cloudless sky the Oxfordshire beech woods glowed, each leaf seeming almost transparent; the grey-green boles looking as if they had been polished; the carpet of countless autumns rustling as I followed a woodland path. Unaccustomed to seeing anyone except a gamekeeper, the birds flitted across the way, though whether from fear or from curiosity I could not tell. Several landed on a nearby tree, whence they watched me with silent suspicion. The squirrels, however, were not silent; they squawked, and one of them followed me overhead, leaping from branch to branch.

How ageless a wood can seem. I first walked that way half a century ago, yet nothing appeared to have changed. I found the same fresh foliage, the same russet carpet, the same blithe birdsong. For all I knew, the squirrel that followed me now was the one that had followed me then. Even the saplings might have been the same Peter Pans, destined never to grow old.

When at last I sighted my friend's hilltop cottage, the sound of an axe suggested that he was indeed alive; but when I walked up the garden path a youth appeared. 'Want to see me?' he asked.

'Well,' I said, 'I'd hoped to see . . . er . . .'

'Uncle?'

'*Your* uncle?'

'Great-uncle, actually.'

'But he's no longer here,' I concluded.

'Not yet,' came the reply. 'five o'clock he gets back from work.'

'Work?' I was amazed. 'But he must be nearly eighty.'

'Eighty-two,' the youth amended.

'Anyway, I'm glad to know he's still so active. Five o'clock, you say? Unfortunately, I can't wait till then. I've left the car several miles away. Are you on a visit?'

'No I live here. Got a job at a farm in the valley. Uncle does odd jobs for the Honourable.'

'Am I correct in thinking she's the squire's daughter?'

'By rights she ought to be the squire, but nowadays the house is a trade union rest home. What a carry-on, eh? You should hear uncle's views about it.'

Myself, I chose to ignore the subject, but was glad to learn that the old man shared the cottage with a young relative of similar outlook. Then the clock called 'Cuckoo' three times, whereupon the youth said: 'Care for a cup of tea. It'd be an excuse for me to have one.'

Indoors, I noticed very little change. A wad of newspaper still kept the rocking-chair on a more or less even keel; the same sooty kettle hung above a log fire; the same tea caddy showed Queen Victoria at her diamond jubilee. 'And,' I asked, 'is that the same cat?'

'Mabel? Oh ah. Near twenty years old is Mabel. A bit stiff in the hindquarters, but otherwise okay. You won't find no mice here.' He poured the tea. 'Milk and sugar?'

'Thank you. May I ask your name?'

'Sam,' he replied, passing the cup. 'Hope it's not too sweet. Uncle and me we both like sugar.'

After a second sip I said: 'Were you born in these parts?'

'No,' he replied. His father drove a bus in London, but his mother used to bring him here during school holidays. 'Whenever I woke up,' he remembered, 'I heard the birds. I liked the people, too. Mum said I even began to speak the way they do. Anyhow, I went to night classes and learned a bit about farming. Only from books, mind. Then uncle got me a job here. The boss is okay. A real gentleman.'

'Do you like the cottage?' I asked.

Without answering, Sam glanced at the cuckoo clock, the brass-studded bellows, the sooty kettle, the tasselled table-cloth, the purring cat. 'One of these days,' he began, then halted.

'I hope you will,' I remarked, reading his unspoken thoughts. 'Your great-uncle would like to think the place was in good hands. Meantime,' I stood up, 'I must be on my way.'

'Far to go?'

'Far enough. Through the woods at Homer and then to Checkendon.'

'A nice walk in this weather,' Sam said, opening the door.

While escorting me down the path, he paused to admire the valley far below. 'The corn's coming on fine,' he observed. 'At harvest time it makes a real picture.' Waving his hand from right to left, he added: 'You can't see it, of course, but over there . . .'

'Lies Oxford,' I agreed.

'So you know?'

'I also know the hill from which you can see the tops of the college towers. As you say, it's a real picture.'

'Anyway,' he shook hands, 'it's been nice meeting you. Only the other day uncle mentioned you. "It's a long time since he called," he said.'

'Too long, and nowadays too far from my home. But tell him I hope to be in these parts before the winter. If I am, I'll certainly call.'

'Any time after five o'clock,' Sam reminded me. 'And once again, thanks for coming.'

Maids of All Work

William Cobbett, son of a Surrey smallholder, felt an especial fondness for his own kind, the farm-hands, whom he called 'the lads of the land'. I feel an especial fondness for the country gentry, the squires and squireens, to whom I dedicate this brief account of their role in English history.

The mediaeval word 'squire' is comparable with the French

esquier, and the various enlargements of its meaning are a précis of the squirearchy itself. In 1645 the word came to mean the owner of a country estate. Thirty years later it meant the principal landowner in a parish or district. In 1809 the Irish were using 'squireen' to connote the gentry who held relatively small estates. Squires achieved prominence during the early Middle Ages, when men of local standing were invited—and sometimes compelled—to ensure that the King's pleas were duly submitted for trial before the itinerant justices. In 1360 these keepers of the peace were empowered to imprison indicted felons; in 1388, under the name of Justices of the Peace, they were required to hear cases four times a year, whence the quarter sessions.

During the sixteenth century a JP's duties were extended to include the suppression of riots, the regulation of wages, the supervision of weights and measures, and sundry other obligations, which caused the Justices to be dubbed 'The Tudor maids of all work'. Noblemen being considered too high, and merchants too low, a large part of local government fell to the gentry, and never more heavily than during a crisis. The Armada, the threat of invasion by Napoleon, the Chartist riots . . . all saw the squires as leaders of rural England, without whose energetic ingenuity the central government might have succumbed to foreign invasion or internal anarchy. During the Napoleonic wars, for example, the Exmoor squires planned a scorched earth policy whereby, if the French did invade, crops were to be razed, livestock destroyed, and women and children evacuated from the danger zones.

The squires' heydays lasted until the beginning of the twentieth century, whereafter many landowners lost their social influence and sometimes their estates also, crippled by taxation. Having sold family heirlooms and treasures, some squires fulfilled a prophecy made by Chief Justice Carew: 'I suppose there is no man that hath any apprehension of gentry and nobility but his affections stand to the continuance of a noble name and house, and he would take hold of any twig or twine-thread to uphold it.'

Partly from lack of money and partly from lack of inclination, the lesser country gentry seldom visited London. Some of the eighteenth-century squires spoke with a regional accent, though others, as graduates of Oxford or Cambridge, were more urbane. Nevertheless, they tended to send their sons to the local grammar school, where they themselves were educated. The descendants of those men may still be found. Some of them either inherited or acquired a baronetcy and perhaps a fortune; others, with a pedigree spanning six centuries, reside on their modest estates, content to serve on the Bench, in the harvest field, and at parish meetings. English literature abounds in squires. Thackeray's Sir Pitt Crawley, one of the wealthier sort, was a poor specimen, and Dickens' Sir Lester Dedlock was hardly more endearing. Goldsmith's Tony Lumpkin, a boorish fellow, was most unlike Squire Allworthy and Flora Thompson's Victorian lord of the manor, a generous man, who agreed with his Sussex contemporary, Wilfred Scawen Blunt:

> Nor hath the world a better thing,
> Though one should search it round,
> Than thus to live one's own sole king
> Upon one's own sole ground.

A village without a squire is a village without a leader, for who nowadays looks to the parson ('He earns less than a garage hand') or to the local council ('Pack of nincompoops, some of 'em'). The businessman who regards his estate solely as an investment, to be sold or leased at the highest possible price, can never replace the squire who was born to the manor and sees it as an inheritance which he will bequeath to his heirs. Such a one was the squire of Southlands, who, said Richard Jefferies, cultivated his land well, with proper regard for his employees.

Even today there are villages—Great Tew in Oxfordshire is an example—which keep something of the dignity and neatness of Great Tew when Lucius Cary maintained the manor house as a meeting place for poets and scholars. Ben Jonson was among the guests who stayed there, relishing the erudite talk and well-stocked library. One bishop declared that he had learned more at Great Tew than at Oxford. From their mediaeval rise to their twentieth-century decline, the best of the squires have tallied with Tennyson's poem:

> And thus he bore without abuse
> The grand old name of gentleman,
> Defiled by every charlatan,
> And soiled by all ignoble use.

In the Combe

There is a combe below the house, with a stream flowing through it. In some places the sides of the combe are so steep that to scramble on all fours is easier than to walk upright. The far side of the combe's southern end is planted with conifers, but the northern half is pasture leading to a small area of larch and beech, now wearing the full glory of their May-time green. Somewhere in the combe a badger lives. One night I almost bumped into him. He has been seen in a lane on the far side of my lower field, and last month I noticed his tracks beside a gate. Rabbits, too, live in the combe. Since the dog always fails to catch them, I share the pleasures of the chase without inflicting pain (for all we know, rabbits are aware of their ability to outstrip most dogs; they may even enjoy exercising that ability). Rooks occupy the northern end of the combe, near enough to be heard, yet far enough not to seem loud. An owl lives somewhere near the rocks, uttering calls which echo eerily after dark.

At least one fox inhabits the combe; and he, too, heightens the stillness by disturbing it. Some people claim that they can distinguish a dog fox's bark from a vixen's, but I never could. In September, when cubbing begins, hounds meet at a farm in the next parish and they seldom fail to flush the combe. Whenever that happens, mounted followers wait beside the stream, leaving the pack and the huntsman to crackle and

IFW

crunch through an acre of briar and weed that has lain unchecked for decades. At such times my own dog must be confined to the house because he is a Jack Russell, a type that was bred for the hunt by the Rev. Jack Russell, who mastered his own pack and was vicar of Swimbridge, less than a dozen miles from the combe. The wood below the house contains squirrels which likewise cause the dog to run amok. When they leap from branch to branch, Jack stands at the base of the tree, barking and baffled. Pheasants from a large estate visit the combe, offering yet another challenge when the dog watches them rise with a shrill whirring. Frogs are non-paying guests in the fishpond beside the roses in the garden. At certain seasons their midnight croaking becomes either an irritant or a lullaby. I like better the thrushes and blackbirds. During July their music dwindles, but on wild winter days the missel-thrush sings while a gale threatens to sweep him from his perch. In May, of course, birdsong reaches the peak of its crescendo.

The district was described by an eminent historian, the Hon. Sir John Fortescue, whose family still owns part of the combe. Fortescue's book about stag-hunting mentions 'a great hill range towering above us. Here we are really in a stronghold of the red deer, the Bray Valley coverts.' Exmoor, in fact, is the largest English habitat of Britain's largest mammal, the wild red deer. When Beatrix Potter visited the moor she reported that 'a herd of thirty-one crossed into the valley the night before, and are living in Horner Woods'. Deer do not live in the combe, but they sometimes forage there. Glancing up from my desk the other day, I saw three hinds ambling across the pasture between the two plantations, damaging the trees by nibbling the bark and the buds. These deer can be very destructive. They will flatten a cornfield by rolling in it and they will ruin a crop of swedes by taking a bite from each one. As with the badgers, so with the stags . . . I have almost bumped into them. It happened late at night while I was walking in a mist on the moorland lane from Luccumbe to Dunkery Beacon. Suddenly, through the gloom, I sighted the hindquarters of a stag. For a moment we both halted in mutual amazement; then the stag bounded from the lane into the heather. I assumed that a headwind and my crêpe soles had hindered him from either hearing or scenting me.

Richard Jefferies' Exmoor book, *Red Deer*, evokes the spaciousness that can be seen from the summit of the combe: 'These hills', he remarked, 'seem only a mile or two away . . . but on going towards them, the table-land suddenly sinks into a deep combe, when it is apparent that the moor which looked so level is really the top of the hill. The combe has to be descended, and ascended, and after five miles' walking very little progress has been made.' Jefferies referred several times to the size of the moor, which may cause a stranger to underestimate the distances: 'The country is very deceptive, much wider and more difficult than it looks. The expanse confuses the eye, and will not allow it to judge distances.' Such deceptiveness is especially conspicuous between Bagworthy Water and Brendon Two Gates, where Hoccombe Combe and Lank Combe lead to other skylines. Despite continual reclamation by farmers, several tracts of the moor still tally with Jefferies' description a century ago: 'One vast breadth of wild, open, and treeless country reaches in every direction.'

Stags, missel-thrushes, seagulls, blackbirds, owls, frogs, rooks, rabbits, badgers, foxes, goldfish, kestrels, woodpeckers, squirrels all live in or close to the combe; a mixed bag indeed, some of whose habits may offend, yet if the creatures are left in peace they usually seem content to remain so. You will never find a gang of robins attacking another gang of robins, nor six squirrels attacking half-a-dozen of their own kind. The teeth and claws of wild animals are as a rule red from hunger or from self-defence against a single predator. It is only human beings who kill with malice aforethought and after careful planning.

I have forgotten to mention the primroses. They abound beside the banks of the stream in the combe; they line every lane for many miles around; and on the slopes of my own small fields they are nosegays and eyegays, a source of unaffected pleasure.

6

Sabrina Fair

I was lately in the West Midlands, feeling dispirited by the towns there, both new and old, which stood like hideous monuments on the grave of farmland. Between Kidderminster and Bridgnorth, where the farmland remained alive and healthy, I sighted a signpost whose single place-name evoked pleasant memories of an earlier visit long ago. My first reaction was: 'No. Never go back. Everything changes, always for the worse. Be content with pleasant memories.' My second reaction was: 'Yes. You must go back. The changes will make the memories seem even more pleasant.' So I did go back, following a lane through country as green as June could paint it.

After about two miles the lane descended quite steeply, past apple orchards and a fieldful of lambs. Then came a sharp bend, and I entered Upper Arley, a village beside the Severn in Worcestershire. Nothing, it seemed, had changed. There they still shone, the red-brick and sandstone cottages astride a little cliff above the river. The church was unchanged, alone on a knoll. Even more remarkable, the two lovers were there—they, or someone very like them, whom I had seen all those years ago—not a day older, still sauntering hand-in-hand beside the water. No less remarkable, Izaak Walton was there, looking rather younger than when he, or someone very like him, had said: 'There's eels 'ere, and trouts, too.' Granted, the ferry had vanished, but the venerable ferryman flourished, or so they told me.

Of course, some things really had changed, though few of

them for the worse, so far as I could see. The miniature post office-cum-shop combined modern hygiene with old-fashioned rusticity. The three or four new houses were built to designs and of materials which merged with their older neighbours. Only the new bridge offended, a poker-faced metal thing. Having crossed the bridge, I looked back at Arley, as pretty a picture as exists anywhere beside Britain's longest river . . . a cluster of cottages, a church, an inn, and behind them the pastures climbing to a tree-topped skyline from which, across the water, I could see another tree-topped skyline, the remnants of Wyre Forest, a haunt of the Weogran tribe that gave its name to Worcester. I once met three charcoal-burners in Wyre Forest, and also a broom-squire or besom-maker whose grandfather had seen a black grouse there.

Back at Arley again, I had a word with the lone angler, who said: 'It isn't always so peaceful. You've arrived at the right time, early mid-week before the holidays start. But if you came back in August . . . cars, cars, cars.' Heeding his words, I made hay before the sun shone too brightly. Along the sandy shore I strolled and thence onto the narrow lane, past flower-filled gardens and picture-postcard cottages. Ten minutes later I rejoined the main road, harried by lorries and cars.

Returning home a few days later, I passed the signpost again. This time I said: 'Don't try your luck too far. Keep the memories pleasant.' Nevertheless, I did try my luck. Along the lane I went, away from the shrill stench of vehicles, into sunshine and birdsong, past the apple blossom and the lambs and the church, down to the Severn, Milton's 'Sabrina Fair'. Would the miracle be repeated? Yes, or almost Yes, for I found two cars instead of one, and three visitors instead of none. But the lovers were still there, and so was Izaak Walton. 'Any luck?' I asked him. His reply was confident rather than confirmatory: 'There will be. There will.'

As my previous visit had been brief, I now decided to linger in the sunny quietude, all the more so because I felt an affinity with the river, having once tracked it from the Severn Sea to the source on Plynlimmon. Crossing the ugly bridge, I soon reached the Harbour Inn, formerly a port-of-call for bargemen outward bound from Bristol or homeward for Bewdley. There I braced myself against an undoubted change for the worse, because a derelict railway lay only a few hundred yards uphill. 'It will be sad,' I said, 'to see the rail-less cutting and the crumbling station.' I reached the railway bridge, peered over the parapet, and was so astonished by what I saw that for several moments I suffered a topsy-turvy *déjà vu.* The track was not rail-less (on the contrary, the lines gleamed blue-grey in the sun) nor was the station crumbling (it looked as though it had just been built and was awaiting the first train). The endearingly Victorian booking office, the signal box, the rolling stock, the gates, the forecourt, the flower beds . . . all, like the track itself, were in good condition. Then two pleasant men from Solihull arrived, who told me (what I had already guessed) that the station and several miles of track had been restored by steam enthusiasts and were now plying profitably as a tourist attraction with express locomotives and a restaurant car. Had I arrived at a later hour on a later day I would have heard the clank of a lowered signal, the unforgettable puffing, the steam sidling from a gland, and perhaps the porter saying to the fireman: 'Good growing weather, Bert. How's your peas looking? And what's the news from Bridgnorth?' It is almost impossible for young people to understand what a boon the bye-lines were, before the coming of cars and buses. To visitors from afar they offered a cheaper and quicker access than did a horse-hauled vehicle from the main line station twenty miles away. To local people they offered easy access to the nearest market town, and were moreover a grapevine as well as a lifeline.

So there it was, a pleasant memory twice revived; Arley Station and the young lovers and Izaak Walton. Shall I ever return again? That would indeed be to try my luck. But I may return, playing for safety by arriving at seven o'clock on a June morning.

Gardening

When E. V. Lucas visited Linfield sixty years ago he rated a house there, called East Mascalls, as 'the most beautiful timbered house in Sussex'. Were he alive to-day, he might rate Linfield itself as one of the most beautiful villages in Sussex. Visitors tend to foregather at the lower end of Linfield, where several old houses overlook a duck pond, yet almost every residence in the village is a period piece, creating an ensemble of timber and stone and brick. After assessing each house, I decided that at least three of them tied for first prize.

At a house beside the pond I noticed an elderly gardener scuffing a lawn with a besom broom, graceful as a sixteenth-century courtier performing a pavane. Adam, they say, was Earth's first gardener: 'And the Lord God planted a garden eastward of Eden; and there he put the man whom he had framed.' Francis Bacon believed that a garden offers 'the purest of all human pleasures. It is the greatest refreshment to the spirits of man; without which, buildings and palaces are but gross handyworks . . .' John Evelyn, whose garden was renowned throughout England, declared: 'no man can be very miserable that is master of a garden . . .'. Gilbert White, who prized his gardener as much as he prized his garden, reported that the former felt very sad when a favourite tortoise wandered off and never returned:

> He has forgot the hangers to repeat
> The accent of his sad regret . . .

During World War II another famous gardener, V. Sackville-West, consoled herself, and many more besides, by composing a long poem on the subject:

> Small pleasures must correct great tragedies,
> Therefore of gardens in the midst of war
> I boldly tell.

On any list of vocations which foster serenity and satisfaction, the role of a professional gardener stands high. Evelyn, whose own skill as a gardener was a source of wonder to his friends, thought so well of the craft that he sketched a variety of implements, from spades and sieves to rollers and rakes, which he proposed to publish in his *Elysium Brittanorum*, a treatise he never completed. I have known several professional gardeners, each of whom agreed that he would gladly spend his life again at the same occupation. Between the professional gardener and the amateur stand the odd-jobbers who combine local lore with trial-and-error. Such a one was Joe, a rubicund little man, who tended my grandfather's garden in north Buckinghamshire. Even as a child, I questioned some of Joe's pronouncements, notably his wish to fell a splendidly umbrageous tree whose upper branches almost touched a verandah above the drawing room. Since my grandfather admired the tree, Joe tried to suborn my grandmother by saying: 'Mark my words, ma'am, you won't ever git nothing to grow beside them French windows, not until you hax thart old tree. It's bin 'ere even longer nor wart oi 'ave, and it's done a deal less good and a soight more 'am.' Grandmother, however, had spent many years in India, and possessed a fair knowledge of exotic trees and shrubs. In order to overawe Joe she would cite the tree's botanical name, *Populus tremula.* I once overheard him remark to the postman: 'Th'old lady calls it a popular trembler, but oi says it's only a 'haspen.'

Grandmother in her age developed a stoop, but was not deterred from dibbling among the plants with a very small hoe on a very long stick. Perhaps because the stick kept her so far away from the plants, Joe sometimes found it necessary to say: 'Them weeds, ma'am, are—or *was*—next month's wallflowers. And you 'aven't exacly improved the asters, 'ave you?'

Although Joe never got his way with the tree, he did succeed in another matter, for he set some tall and fast-growing shrubs near the red-brick wall of what he called 'The fruitery', and there, undisturbed, he would sit smoking his pipe, whereof the acrid smoke was presumed to come from a bonfire. The garden itself being modest rather than immense, Joe had ample time for blending horticultural with domestic tasks which included cleaning the shoes, the windows, and the bicycles. Fancying himself as a builder, he would scale the roof in order to secure a slate or to adjust the gutter. He was extremely proud of his 'fruitery', though the domain scarcely deserved its sobriquet, and I cannot remember seeing anything except one pear tree, two apple trees, and a tangle of redcurrant bushes encircled by a few lettuces and marrows. The apples were conserved on the topmost storey of the house, which contained a second bathroom and three attics, two of the latter being sparsely furnished for ourselves, the grandchildren. The third attic was not furnished at all, and in it, on newspapers laid across bare boards, Joe arranged his apples, as in Drinkwater's poem:

> At the top of the house apples are laid in rows,
> And the skylight lets light in, and those
> Apples are deep-sea apples.

Every calling has its defects and defectors. No doubt the Newgate Calendar does include the names of gardeners who emulated Adam's greed and Eve's *faux-pas*. In my own experience, however, the professional gardener is an upright man who finds unfailing delight in his ability to propagate beauty and nourishment, and so to tend them that they excel the achievements of lesser practitioners. Such men are as a rule healthy and long-lived. Their lot contents them. They envy no man, least of all his fame or fortune. Gardeners on great estates have assured me that they would positively dislike to live as lords of all they survey. 'We weren't born to it', they said, 'and we're too old to be bred to it. Besides, if we did employ gardeners we'd cease to *be* gardeners.'

Foresters work for a future which they may never see; newspaper reporters work for a future which becomes the past before they ever predict it; but a gardener—whether professional or amateur—works for a future which, since it lies just around the calendar, he may reasonably expect to enjoy, all the more so because his garden offers a perpetual challenge and a perennial fulfilment.

Down to the Sea

Shipbuilding is not usually regarded as rural craftsmanship. One thinks rather of drab streets leading to grimy shunting yards overlooking mud-banked estuaries under a pall of smoke. But not all ships are large, and until relatively recent times many of them were sailing vessels that were launched in sight of hayricks and sheepfolds. A few such yards still thrive, though none will ever again build a Medway Bawley nor a Lancashire Nobby. All round the coast, and well within living memory, such yards produced their own type of boat . . . Hastings Lugger, Thames Barge, Falmouth Quay Punt, Itchen Cutter, Shetland Sixern, Northumberland Coble. All, or nearly all, have vanished, for Progress has removed the speed-limit on a crescendo which Defoe described two centuries ago: 'The Face of Things so often alters, and the Situation of Affairs in this Great British Empire gives such new Turns, even to Nature itself, that there is Matter of new Observation every Day presented to the Traveller's Eye.'

The smallest boatyard I ever visited was also the most rural.

It lay between the blue waters and green hills of St Just-in-Roseland, across the bay from Falmouth, where you could bespeak a mahogany dinghy with paddles and brass rowlocks, costing £1 per foot; in other words, £7 for a pram whose like would now strain even a rich man's purse. Elderly people will remember the Plymouth Stone Barges that worked from several west country ports. As their name implies, the vessels carried stone from the quarries, but they also took a mixed cargo. Being flat-bottomed, they remained upright on the seabed at low tide. Some of them had a rounded stern, others a shallow transom. Their mainmast was stepped well forward, leaving clear space for hatch and hold. Fitted with an engine, one of the barges was carrying naval supplies at Plymouth during the 1960s.

I often wonder what has happened to the countrymade vessel which I saw at Fleetwood many years ago. She was a Lancashire Nobby or Morecambe Bay Prawner, thirty-one feet long, with a beam of almost ten feet, yet drawing only four feet of water. The bow—almost vertical at the stem head—curved steeply into the keel line just above the waves. The stern was a low and elliptical counter, which meant that the boat seemed in danger of being pooped when moving fast. The low freeboard certainly set the gunwale awash. Rigged as cutters, these craft had a long bowsprit and a boomed mainsail. At Glasson, the port of Lancaster, an old sailor told me of a Nobby that had been converted into an ocean-going yacht. A retired naval officer lately assured me that in 1950 or thereabouts he sighted a Loch Fyne Skiff under canvas on the Clyde. I envied him because I had seen only a picture of those fishing vessels, formerly a feature of the west coast of Scotland. Seldom exceeding thirty-five feet in length, the Skiffs were as open as a Viking longboat; even the largest had only a partly-decked cuddy. The raked mast was stepped well forward, carrying a lugsail. A jib could be hoisted from the bowsprit. In 1939 several Loch Fyne Skiffs received an engine and were adapted to serve as minesweepers.

During the 1930s I noticed a smack in Emsworth Harbour, where the editor of a Hampshire newspaper introduced me to a veteran who had helped to build such boats. It seems that the Emsworth Smack was designed by a man named Foster, owner of a small fishing fleet, who wished to sail beyond the confines of Chichester Harbour. His own boats, sixty feet long, looked rather like a pilot cutter. In 1901 he designed the *Echo*, then rated as the finest of all British fishing boats under sail, or so they said at Emsworth. Although she was one hundred feet long, with a beam of twenty-one feet, she drew less than nine feet of water. Under full canvas, with an auxiliary steam engine, she attained fourteen knots. Some of the Emsworth Smacks were working from Newhaven until the eve of World War II. When these and other sailing ships disappeared, they took with them a breed of men and a type of navigation that are not to be found among modern sailors, not even among our fisherfolk. Seafarers at the beginning of the twentieth century had no radio, no radar, no depth-sounder, no gale warning. They relied on barometers and lifelong understanding of their native waters. Many of the boats were built for the sort of skipper whose son was the mate and whose grandson was the cabin boy. Sometimes the wife sailed with them, and in a crisis she steered while the men wrestled with a broken boom.

New needs create new skills, but they also destroy old ones. If the remnants of a once-great British fishing fleet are to save themselves from foundering, they must keep pace with the latest technology and the scurviest tricks of common marketeers. Nevertheless, it is natural to mourn the decay of estuaries and small harbours which offered a livelihood to men who were proud of their hazardous calling, and reluctant to follow any other. Nowadays those rural landfalls rely on building and maintaining pleasure boats. As for the great ports of London and Liverpool and Bristol, their dockers and stevedores have almost scuttled them. The empty berths mock Masefield's vision of

> The great street paved with water,
> filled with shipping,
> And all the world's flags flying,
> and the seagulls dipping.

Chiltern Beech Woods

The Chiltern Hills of Oxfordshire and Buckinghamshire are famous for their beech woods. Defoe described as 'almost incredible' the quantity of Chiltern beeches that were sold to the furniture trade or as domestic fuel: 'Yet', he added, 'so is the country overgrown with beech in these parts, that it is bought very reasonable, nor is there like to be a scarcity of it for time to come.' Unfortunately, the area of those beech woods has been reduced by landowners who nowadays plant quick-profit conifers. Another destroyer is the traffic that causes wayside coverts to be felled, thereby confirming the truth of William Blake's remark: 'The tree which moves some to tears of joy is in the eyes of others only a green thing which stands in the way.' Since I lived in the Chilterns for many years, I make a point of returning there in June, while the leaves are fresh, and again in October, while they are flamboyant. This time I went to a hill near my old home on the outskirts of Prestwood, where the view has hardly changed in half a century. Ahead and on the right, other hills appeared, topped with beech woods and bluebells. The weather was idyllic. The sun shone, the birds sang, the lambs bleated.

The lane soon dipped to join a wider road, and by turning right and then left I reached a second lane, which toiled uphill, passing yet another beech wood paved with bluebells. On the edge of the wood I noticed some rusty barbed wire with which I had tried to deter motorists from driving over the blue carpet. I never succeeded. Year after year the vandals uprooted my efforts to protect the property of a negligent farmer. Fortunately, the bluebells were as profuse as ever. In fact, they composed a coloured poem. Like vintage wine, however, poetry should be offered sparingly, in the knowledge that (to mix a metaphor) it is not everyone's cup of tea; but when the sun shines on a bluebell wood in June, only a total abstainer will refuse to sip. I therefore sampled six lines:

Oak is crowned the King of trees,
Hawthorn yields a coloured scent,
Willow whispers to the breeze,
Cherry whitely welcomes Lent:
But in spring the Beech is seen
Undeniably a Queen.

Wandering among familiar places, I succumbed to nostalgia, especially when I passed a solitary house in the upper part of the wood. Many times I had called there, but were I to call now, the occupants would not know me, nor would they know the sculptor who used to live there, nor the scholar who came after. However, the larks were so loud that only a chronic depression could have prevailed against their music. Out of the corn they sprang, and then, as the air took them, down came those melodies which surely express something more lyrical than territorial claims. Near the brow of the hill I recognized an old acquaintance who was evidently astonished to meet me. 'Oi 'aven't seen you for ages,' he exclaimed. 'We all thought you was dead an' gorn.'

'On the contrary,' I replied, 'I'm very much alive, especially in this weather.'

'Well, well.' The old man could not conceal his astonishment. 'We all thought you was . . .' he checked his candour. 'Them others,' he said, glancing at the solitary house, 'they really 'ave gorn. Ah, and one of 'em's dead.' At that point he looked defiant. 'But oi aren't dead. Wart's more, oi don't bloody well intend to be, not yetawhoile. And oi'll tell you something else . . . oi 'aven't packed up work noither. Oi still does a bit of obloiging when oi feels loike it.' This time he glanced apprehensively over his shoulder. 'Not that you need tell th' income tax. They take far too much as it is. Well, well. Oi really did think you was . . .' Again he checked himself. 'You've got a new dog, oi see. Th' old 'un were a Lakeland, warn't 'ee?'

'He was.'

'And then one afore 'im were a spaniel. And thart's going back a bit, eh? Well, well. Oi'll 'ave to tell the missus about this. She often wonders 'ow you're gitting on.' The part-time obliger quizzed the sun. 'Oi must be gitting on, too. Oi promised to mow the lawn for someone. If it didn't mean doing myself out of a job, oi'd tell th' old girl, "If you was to mow it yourself you'd be a soight more hactive nor wart you are".' He then shook hands and descended the hill, still muttering, 'Well, well.'

Presently I reached a footpath overlooking Little Hampden and its whitewashed church beside a steep lane that ends among beech woods. I was, in fact, encircled by beech woods, some of them in the valley, others on the skyline, all at the peak of perfection. The only visible buildings were the church, a farmhouse, and a couple of cottages; everything else was either farmland or woodland. Resting on a stile, I remembered that beech woods during winter are as handsome as during spring; and with the remembrance I took another sip:

> Poplar preens its symmetry,
> Guelder grants a wayside rose,
> Holly lights a Christmas Tree,
> Blackthorn scatters April snows:
> But the leafless Beech is still
> Peerless on a Chiltern hill.

Nightpiece

When June justifies its glorious reputation, the cool of the evening comes as a welcome respite from the heat of the day. Fourteen hours ago, at seven o'clock in the morning, the sun had already bestowed a caress which at noon became a sting, causing the haymakers to shelter under a tree. At teatime even the seaside sunbathers showed signs of wilting under the glare. Three hours later it was still too hot for comfortable walking. At nine o'clock in the evening the midges continued to bite, hovering like a swarm of miniature bees; but now at last the sun is setting. The heat and burden have slipped away, like a yoke from weary shoulders.

Somewhere in the combe below this garden a blackbird is singing, not indeed with the rapture of his sunrise serenade, yet with a serenity which the earlier song lacked. Farther away, in a hilltop wood, the rooks maintain their nightly noise while moment by moment the light ebbs westward where a few pink patches still attest the day's decline. The moon is up, attended by stars that percolate a steely stare among the trees.

The blackbird is silent now. Through the dusk I can just see him fly away to roost. In the combe, hundreds of feet below, a stream proceeds, self-mesmerized as in a dream, repetitively reciting the same refrain over and over again as if striving to make its perfection even more flawless. Like the wild rose that glimmers in the twilight, that stream and that bird are as ancient as de la Mare's pedigree:

> Oh, no man knows
> Through what centuries
> Roves back the rose.

The pink patches are fading until only an amber aura remains, seemingly the reflection from a furnace below the horizon. Gone now the intense heat and the nibbling midges; but not yet gone a trace of warmth in the field-gate on which I am leaning. Half a mile away, from the combe's deepest corner, an owl is answered by a fox that barks thrice. On the far side of the stream the sheep shine in moonlight, grazing inch by inch like moving mushrooms.

When we speak of silence we forget that utter soundlessness is very rare and may in fact never occur on this planet. We hear our own breathing, and the air itself moves albeit so stealthily that we often fail to detect the stirrings. In deep country, however, stillness and quietude are common; yet even tonight—when, as we say, the world seems to be asleep—even tonight and even in this deep country, a keen ear detects stray sounds. Almost at my feet something is rustling through the grass; a beetle, perhaps, or a field mouse foraging for food. Then a fragment of leaf falls from a sycamore, and two twigs touch each other, nudged by a breeze too frail to make itself felt on my face. Now I cannot hear any sound at all, not even my own breathing. If I have patience and listen intently I may soon . . . yes, there goes that owl again, waking the whole combe or so it seems, whereupon a bird utters its own protest against neighbours who disturb the night. But the disturbance is brief. Owl and fox and bird fall silent and remain so.

The dog has suddenly stiffened, uncertain whence comes the sound which my own ears have failed to catch. Now his head swivels due south, and presently I hear a neighbouring farmer climbing homeward to a house beyond the hill. His collie and the Jack Russell greet amicably, bitch to dog. Our greetings sound loud above the stillness.

'Lovely night.'

'You'm right. Bids well for the hay. That shower yesterday did a power o' good. You out for a stroll?'

'I am. It was too hot earlier on.'

'Ah, and they damned midges were terrible busy.' He gave his nape a reminiscent scratch. 'Ah well, I must be getting along else the missus will begin to wonder what's happened. Goodnight.'

'And to you.'

His footsteps can be heard until, at a bend in the lane, he opens a gate and takes a short cut across the fields. I hear the gate-latch fall into place and then, from the next field, the sound of a metal gate being opened and shut. After that the stillness seems eternal, and through it I return home, stepping on moonbeams that slant across the lane and are filtered onto the drive.

The scene itself, of moonlight and shadow, has a counterpart in the music of Debussy's *Images*. Were the stream louder it would recall *Cathédrale Engloutie* as vividly as the moonbeams do recall *Clair de Lune.* Stravinsky classified such melodies as 'mood music', yet they are something more than ornamentation, for they revive and sharpen our own pleasure in beauty *per se*, of which the world does not offer so much that we can dismiss a June night as mere pastiche, a kind of child's play, long since outgrown by practical men. Evanescence did not deter Robert Bridges from his own quest for beauty:

I too will something make
And joy in the making
Although tomorrow it seem
Like the empty words of a dream
Remembered on waking.

7

Storm

We knew what to expect, but we did not expect what we witnessed. None of us, in fact, had ever before seen such a sky. Half of it was cloudlessly blue, crowned by a sun that scorched us as we sat in the garden; the other half glowered greyer than the North Sea. The oppressive atmosphere foretold a storm.

'Until the sun does disappear', one of us said, 'we may as well stay where we are.' So stay we did, watching the clouds approach. Then, as the first raindrop dimpled the fishpond, we collected our chairs and went indoors, glancing westward when thunder rumbled in the distance. 'If it gets any darker', somebody remarked, 'we'll have to switch the lights on.'

All descriptions of a thunderstorm lie under the shadow of Beethoven's 'Pastoral' Symphony, which marvellously imitates the arrival and departure of the sound and fury. Nevertheless, language offers its own account of the lull before, the darkness during, and the sunlight after, a storm. Meanwhile, we flinched as the first streak of lightning suffused the sky with silvery brilliance.

'If you count the number of seconds between the bang and the flash', the youngest of us said, 'you can calculate how far away . . .' The rest of his sentence was cut short by a second rumble, louder and nearer. The rain, by contrast, still dallied, speckling the pond with a few spots that might have been made by the fish themselves, rising to an insect. The next flash was vicious. It zigzagged, causing the telephone to tinkle. Ten seconds later the pond resembled a maelstrom of miniature waterspouts. The lawn hissed, the gutters gushed, the windows streamed. It became so dark that we not only switched on the lights but also drew the curtains together, as though they would lessen the din and deflect the danger.

While admitting that the downpour was needed by parched meadows and depleted reservoirs, we could not help feeling that, unlike Beethoven's storm, this one had outstayed its welcome. For what seemed a claustrophobic eternity the storm hovered overhead, as though hemmed in by the hills. Despite its sturdy walls—nearly two feet wide—the house shook whenever a thunderclap arrived. As for the lightning, we heard, or thought we heard, it hissing, venomous as a snake's forked tongue. Our flagging conversation, repeatedly interrupted by flashes and crashes, became a litany of self-revelation: 'This sort of weather always gives me a headache' . . . 'Of course, nobody minds the thunder, but I did once hear of a golfer who stood under a tree' . . . 'It's bound to go away sometime. Nothing lasts for . . . I say, that one was right overhead. It even made the dog bark' . . . 'If you want to see a real thunderstorm you must visit the tropics.'

Some people still believe that thunder and lightning are caused by two or more clouds colliding, a fallacy at least as old as Lucretius, who propounded it in his poem *De Rerum Natura.* Pooling our own slight understanding of the subject, we agreed that thunderstorms may occur when warm air near the earth is overlaid by colder air, so that moisture begins to form raindrops. These drops cannot fall faster than 17.9 miles an hour, and the flux of hot and cold air causes them to rise as well as to fall. During those fluctuations the raindrops split up, producing small charges of positive electricity in themselves and small charges of negative electricity in the atmosphere. Some flashes of lightning are more than a mile long and are 100,000 amps as against the five amps of domestic light and power.

In the end, of course, the storm did go away, fainter and fainter; then reviving awhile, and finally ending as a murmur. The rain, however, persisted, heavily and without interruption. We therefore kept the lights on and the curtain drawn. Eventually someone exclaimed: 'Listen! It's stopped raining.' We drew back the curtains. 'Look, the sun's trying to shine.' Thankful to escape from an unpleasant interlude, we all trooped outside. Once more we knew what to expect, and once more our expectations did not prevent us from being surprised by what we did see. Summer had been transformed to look like spring, mild and moist and green. So lately shrivelled, the meadows glistened, and the lawn when we crossed it sighed, like one whose thirst has at last been slaked. Trees and shrubs cupped raindrops that might have been dew. Give or take a few browbeaten victims, the flowers no longer drooped, but stood upright on strengthened stalks. Dusty indentations were fulsome puddles. The sky turned blue again, and the sun warmed the soil, this time without scorching it. All the birds were singing again, as though, like the land itself, they, too, had been refreshed. A blackbird led the chorus, descanting from a tree on the far side of the combe. Two thrushes chimed in, one from the wood below the garden, the other from a beech in the drive. Robins we recognized, and wrens and blue-tits, and on the highest bough a two-tone chiff-chaff, perky as a seaman setting the main upper top-gallant. Had a cuckoo called, the analogy with April would have seemed valid. James Thomson described a similar aftermath:

> Nature from the storm
> Shines out afresh . . .
> 'Tis beauty all, and grateful song around.

We ourselves certainly went around, walking the gauntlet of trees that baptized our bare heads; stepping childlike into the newly formed puddles; sharing the general mood of relief and re-invigoration; and having returned to the house, someone exclaimed: 'Good Lord, we didn't switch the lights off.'

A Holiday Mood

Visitors to the countryside cannot help noticing a kind of holiday mood among the local people. The majority of farm folk really do seem to enjoy their work, whether it be mowing a meadow or mending a gate. This impression is caused by a change of scene wherein buildings and noise give way to fields and quietude.

Wherever he goes the visitor will overhear a weather forecast which links a holiday mood with a workaday comment. When the shepherd says to the milk girl: ''Tis warm again, midear,' he will add: 'Let's hope it stays that way till the corn's safely in.' Similarly, the farmer's wife, having said to the postman's sister: 'What a storm it was last night,' will add: 'Just when we were trying to take a second crop of hay.' If they are questioned on the subject, countryfolk may be at a loss to account for an attitude which they acquired in childhood, for although village children seldom run to school gleefully, those who walk thither are conspicuously less snail-like than their town contemporaries. In any part of rural Britain a fine summer morning during termtime will reveal school-bound children picking flowers beside a lane or seeking birds'-nests in a hedge. When they grow up, some of those children will find work in a large town, where it is unlikely that they ever will share a perennial holiday mood. Others, however, may find work near their own parish, where they probably will share such a mood. Thus, while most of the rest of the world is still asleep, a farm-hand swishes through the dew, noting that the last cuckoo has departed or that the first fieldfare has arrived. Scything nettles or shearing sheep, he takes his midday meal at ease, and afterwards rests awhile, supine in the shade.

Farmers lean on a gate, admiring their crops, calculating the likely profit therefrom, and marvelling that anyone should wish to live in a city. Veterans warm their bones in the sun, uttering a platitude as though it were a new discovery: 'Thart old blackbird's fair singing 'is 'ead 'orf' . . . 'Yon brae looks bonnie wi' the heather' . . . 'Rhys Evans, this is the hottest day I can remember since my da's hayrick combusted itself sixty years ago.'

On the coast, the holiday mood is intensified. Bleached by a lifetime of sun and wind, men in blue jerseys and salt-caked seaboots lounge against up-turned dinghies, stroll along sandy beaches, or peer over seething gunwales. Since the ups-and-downs of life are as unpredictable in a village as they are in a town, one must assume that the rural holiday mood is neither an illusion nor an affectation, but arises as a natural response to the environment; and the more widely one travels in Britain, the more firmly one is convinced that the assumption is justified. There are hamlets whose only shopkeeper leaves the door open while he dozes on a bench beside the porch. There are housewives who relax in a deck-chair while the clothes line above them shines like a cluster of small yachts manoeuvring at the start of a race. There are country parsons who, as they visit their flock, give thanks for such a truly pastoral pilgrimage, so different from the missions of a dockland curate. There are country solicitors who, having worked in shirt-sleeves till lunchtime, return to their garden, perhaps to study a document, more likely to mow the lawn or to take a nap. There are country doctors who, as they drive past ripening cornfields, thank their lucky star that they are not practising in an industrial city.

The matter is well illustrated when a certain type of townsman arrives with his family at the holiday cottage. After twenty-four hours of unaccustomed relaxation, the visitors can no longer control their restlessness. As a result, the elderly farm-hand, prodding six cows down the lane, witnesses the hectic activity as Dad cleans the windscreen while several voices call: 'Did anyone remember to switch off the stove?' . . . 'Are you sure you packed the Scotch eggs?' . . . 'Where's that dog got to?' . . . 'Don't let mum drive or we'll never get there.' Rosy as an apple in September, the farm-hand observes the general agitation, the slamming of doors, the roar of the engine. Swaying as leisurely as his herd, he seems amused, and when the noise has faded away he leans against a gate, content to scan the sky and hills above his own patch of paradise. Having ushered in the cows, he walks half a mile to his next task, the scything of a paddock, which he performs with evident satisfaction.

The day's work done, he sits in a cool kitchen, relishing a high tea of fish and scones and jam and cake. As his wife refills the teacups he says: 'They'm a real harum-scarum bunch at that holiday cottage. They don't never come down to breakfast till near ten o'clock, and then they'm away gadding in their motor car.' He shakes his head. 'Yesterday they told me it took 'em nearly an hour to get through Barnstaple. Why, I could walk it quicker.'

At eight o'clock the visitors return, sounding and looking very tired indeed; but at ten o'clock the farm-hand strolls home from The Wheatsheaf, feeling as Milton felt:

> This is the pleasant time,
> The cool, the silent, save when silence yields
> To the night-warbling bird . . .

Names on the Map

The holiday motorist was lost. He was also irritable, perspiring, and so stupid that—had no witnesses been present to corroborate it—I might still disbelieve the saga of his misadventures. Meanwhile, there he stood, on a steep and narrow lane in one of the remotest parts of North Devon, saying to me: 'Which is the best way to Manchester?'

I felt tempted to adapt the reply of an Irish peasant who, when a visitor inquired the way to Dublin, said: 'If it's Dublin you want to get to, this is a terrible bad place to start from.' However, the motorist's plight seemed so pitiful that I did my best to help him, not least because he had already wasted several hours trying to find a friend's house at Downton on Dartmoor; but instead of consulting the map, he consulted his hotel at Totnes, and since there is a Downton within a few miles of Totnes, thither they directed him. The distance between the two Devonshire Downtons is not less than forty slow and sinuous miles. Finally, for reasons which I hesitated to seek, he had got as far as Exmoor, which is indeed a bad starting place for anyone wishing to reach Manchester. Although I drew a sketch map for him, I wonder whether the Mancunian ever found Simonsbath. Mind you, even a map-reader may sometimes need to ask the way. In Lincolnshire I certainly needed to ask the way to Isaac Newton's birthplace, Woolsthorpe, because two villages of that name stood within a few miles of each other. Their proximity astonished me until I remembered that place-names are older than post codes or the habit of travelling faster than a horse can trot.

In years when literacy was for the most part a privilege of clerics, and when nine-tenths of the population seldom ventured far beyond their own villages, it scarcely mattered that two Woolsthorpes stood so close to each other, because strangers very seldom visited them, and local people knew the names of all their inhabitants. Modern travellers, by contrast, are perplexed by such duplication and triplication and quadruplication. For example, there are three Bamptons in England. The largest (or least small) is a Devonshire town with an annual fair whose chief wares are Exmoor ponies. Oxfordshire's Bampton is likewise a small town with an annual fair, for on May Day the Morris dancers meet there to perform their intricate convolutions. Westmorland's Bampton is a village in the Lowther valley, five miles from Shap. Its grammar school, long since defunct, educated a Bishop of London and an Archbishop of Canterbury.

It will surprise many Dark Blues (and many non-Blues also) to learn that England contains two Oxfords; the lesser is in Northumberland. Cambridge goes one better by scoring a hat-trick; the younger offspring being respectively near Southend in Essex and near Stroud in Gloucestershire. The Light Blues almost achieve a quartet because the Gloucestershire Cambridge is quite close to the village of Cam, William Tyndale's boyhood home. There are also a number of quadruplets in British topography. I recall four Bangors (Flintshire, Cardiganshire, Carmarthenshire, County Down) and four Sheltons (Shropshire, Bedfordshire, Nottinghamshire, Norfolk).

Our ancestors did indeed bequeath a splendid legacy of place-names, some of which are lyrical: High Heaven, Christmas Common, Good Easter, Bethlehem, Nightingales, Pity Me, Zeal Monachorum, St Anthony-in-Roseland, Zoy, Foy, Stanton-on-the-Hine-Heath, Wendens Ambo, Kibworth Beauchamp, Saint Columb Major, Indian Queens. Several place-names are comical: Drunken Bottom, Great Snoring, Oh Me Edge, Clock Face, Devil's Beef Tub, Ugley, Chimney, Nad, Tey, Muck. At least a dozen names have a baptismal timbre: Patrick Brompton, Edith Weston, George Green, Mary Tavy, Robin Hood, Burton Agnes, Robert Law, Thomson, Charles, Archdeacon Newton, Parson Grove. Many Cornish place-names are so zany that I once set some of them to their own music:

> Columb, Clether, Clement, Issey,
> Breock, Breward, Ding-Dong, Just;
> Mewgan, Mawgan, Minven, Levan,
> Ive, Portscatho, Roseland, Erth;
> Baragwanath, Trink, Lamorna,
> Plain-an-Gwarry, Come-to-Good.

Elsewhere you will find scores of Uptons or villages standing higher than a near neighbour. Several Uptons append their pedigree, as at Upton Cresset in Shropshire (the manor passed to a Norman, Thomas Cresset) and Upton Grey in Hampshire (whose lord in 1271 was John de Grey). By far the commonest British place-name or prefix is Wood. There are literally hundreds of them, from Woodend in Perthshire and Woodside in Pembrokeshire to Woodseaves in Staffordshire and Woodhouse in Leicestershire. The name itself usually refers to forests in the district because mediaeval Britain contained vast areas of woodland. However, Woodale in Yorkshire means 'wolves' valley', and at other places the names refer to dead timber rather than to standing trees. Two examples are Woodchurch in Cheshire (where the Saxons founded a timber church) and Woodchester in Gloucestershire (Domesday Book called it *Widecestre*, meaning 'Roman fort, either built of wood or set in a wood').

Postmen as well as letter-writers in Merionethshire must often have been misled by two places called Afon Mawddach, each within a short distance of the other. Shropshire has two neighbouring Aldertons; Wiltshire has two neighbouring Allingtons; Lancashire, two neighbouring Bartons; Worcestershire, two neighbouring Churchills; Cumbria, two Crosbys; Cambridgeshire, two Delph Bridges; Durham, two Newfields; Gloucestershire, two Woodmancotes; Sussex, two Trottons; Herefordshire, two Portways; Inverness-shire, two Pabbays; Perthshire, two Beinn Deargs and also two Beinn Odhars . . . and so on until even a sorting-machine suffers from double vision.

The Celtic south-west claims that its place-names are more melodious than those of the Nordic and Germanic regions of England. It may be so, yet Essex, too, can compose a topographical poem: Wingle Tye, Lambkins, Lapwater, Pyrgo, Hobs Aerie, Willingdale Doe, Sible Hedingham, Stoke-by-Clare, Layer Marney, Mardfield Saling, Bradwell-juxta-Coggeshall, Wendens Ambo, Wickham Bishops, Duck's End. On balance, however, Cornwall does contain the cream of Celtic nomenclature. My own recipe concluded thus:

Sancreed, Trencrum, Indian Queens,
Praze-an-Beeble, Zone, Chykembro,
Wheals of Damsel, Rose, and Jewel;
Mawla, Morvah, Marazion,
Amalabrea, Chyandor.

Cats and Dogs

In a comment on cats, Gilbert White remarked how strange it was that they should be so fond of fish. No doubt the fish in my own pond share his surprise. Even the cat may share it, if only because the water level stops him from landing a catch. Other and less domesticated cats hereabouts have been swept away while casting for trout in a river near Brayley Barton.

My first cat, named Mimi, came as a gift when I was still very young. All else about her I have forgotten, except the inconsolable grief of childhood when she wandered off and never came back. The biggest cat I ever saw belonged to a farmer at Copdock in Suffolk, one of whose horses I used to ride. This cat was so massive that it might have passed for a small fox. It often caught a rabbit, and on one occasion it gnawed through the door of a shed in which it had been locked when hounds approached. The farmer told me that no other cat dared to visit the farm.

Ginger, the First, so named for obvious reasons, was acquired many years later, when mice had raided a sack of oats in the barn. He, too, was a formidable warrior, able to catch rabbits. The mice soon disappeared when they discovered his prowess. Refuting the fallacy that all cats and dogs were irreconcilable enemies, Ginger befriended the spaniel, Simon, and would lie beside him in front of the fire. Like Mimi, however, Ginger the First wandered off and never came back. As in childhood, I searched in vain, though not with the same anguish.

During the 1950s, while living in the Chilterns, I found a very small kitten under a hedge, apparently too weak to move. Stunted though it was, the kitten hissed viciously when I tried to lift it. By the time both of us had reached home my hands were covered with tiny scratches. When offered a saucer of milk, the waif drew back and would not touch it. For the next six hours the mewing grew steadily weaker. At about midnight I telephoned the vet, explaining the circumstances and apologizing for what might appear to be undue concern. Half an hour later the vet arrived. 'Exposure and chronic malnutrition,' he said. 'I doubt whether it'll live until the morning.' We therefore agreed to inject a merciful needle. So far from regarding me as a nuisance, the vet approved his mission and declined to charge for it.

A long time elapsed before Ginger the Second joined me at my new home, in response to a challenge from mice that were nesting among some newspapers behind the refrigerator. Like his predecessor, Ginger the Second soon routed the enemy. It so happened that he arrived shortly after I had acquired a Jack Russell puppy which, I hoped, would console me when the Lakeland terrier, already in his seventeenth year, departed this life. How amicably the trio blended. A photograph shows them at feeding time; the veteran sampling the bowl, the puppy sniffing his saucer, the cat waiting for any crumbs that fell from the rich men's table. Like the first of his name, Ginger wandered off and never came back. Was he a victim of the hounds that passed that morning? Was he trapped? Stolen? Killed by a fox? Again I searched the fields, and again they gave no answer to my questions.

The present cat is a prettily marked black-and-white one, which explains why a friend's daughter named him Tinker. Alas, while still a kitten, he slipped from a roof, mewing loudly. The vet diagnosed a spinal injury. 'You mustn't let him move about,' he said. 'If he's kept in a small box for several weeks he may recover.' So, into a small box he went, and out of it, an hour later, he emerged. 'Better to die,' I said, 'than be cooped up in misery.' The gamble succeeded. Today you would not guess that Tinker had injured his spine. Only an expert can detect the slight curvature, and no one at all will deny that he is as active as if he had never slipped. The Lakeland terrier died seven years ago, but the Jack Russell is still in the prime of life, and he and Tinker continue to confound the doctrine of mutual incompatibility. They lie together on the hearth; they sleep within a yard of each other in a shed; they chase the same ball; they make friends with sheep in the upper field. Tinker, in fact, accompanies us on our walk, halting when he reaches the second gate in Farmer Seymour's meadow. On our return he greets us at the fishpond. I am not, of course, suggesting that Tinker and Jack never disagree. When play becomes too rough, the cat extends his claws; when visitors enter the house, the dog demands to receive the first admiring pat. Nevertheless, each seems to know how far he can go without arousing real hostility in the other.

Every farm and most rural families possess a cat, and some people are fonder of cats than they are of dogs. Although cats wander in and out, like guests at a hotel, everyone agrees that they appreciate a kindly household. One farmer assured me that his own cat, having been stolen by gipsies, managed to find its way home during a snowstorm. Tinker himself is now strolling across my shoulder, an affectionate gesture, but not to be interpreted as the devotion with which a dog serves his master.

Leaning on a Bridge

In high summer, when the land looks dusty and thirsty, it is pleasant to seek the cool companionship of water. More fortunate than most, by walking a few miles I can sight the confluence of the Severn Sea and the Atlantic Ocean, and by walking a few hundred yards I can lean on a small bridge, counting the minnows in the stream. It so happens that some of my earliest memories are of a bridge, the one at Crowland in the Lincolnshire Fens, where I spent part of my childhood. So far as I know, Crowland's bridge is unique because it has three lanes, joined together at angles of 120 degrees, each spanning a stream at the junction of the Welland and the Nene. In the year 943 an earlier bridge on the site was described as 'triangulo per aquam de Weland'.

As a schoolboy I used to lean on a hump-backed bridge near Water Eaton in Buckinghamshire. This bridge would have delighted Richard Jefferies's Bevis because it offered water-milling, coarse fishing, and canal cruising in horse-hauled barges on the adjacent waterway. Nowadays I enjoy a half-hour stroll to the moss-mottled bridge marking the boundary between this parish and the next. There, too, a water-mill once served the district, but whereas the Buckinghamshire mill has vanished, the Devonshire mill survives and now generates electricity for the old mill house. This sequestered haven lies at the bottom of a 1-in-3 lane, where the bridge crosses a steam. Despite its sun-trapping situation, the bridge is shaded by trees and therefore remains comparatively cool. Since few folk ever use the lane, I feel no qualms about removing my shoes and socks in order to paddle. The dog prefers to splash under the arch, which is scarcely a yard above the water.

Very different is the bridge across the Severn near Llanidloes, only a few miles from the source on Plynlimon in Wales. Unlike Rome (and also unlike any other Severn bridge), this one really was built in a day. It comprises two planks and a rickety wire handrail, evidently put there by a farmer whose land lay on the opposite bank. Careful not to lean against the handrail, I have several times stood on the bridge, watching the stripling Severn, Britain's longest river, flowing towards Somerset and the sea. The skylines beyond the bridge are ringed with hills and trees, and the lane itself is followed only by local farmfolk and a few pilgrims to the source. Many of the natives speak Welsh, and not only the natives. When a Scottish schoolmaster went in search of bed and breakfast he was heard to say to the manageress of the hotel at Llangurig: 'Oes gennowh whe thin or booyd ta a cletty da?' (in other and more familiar words: 'Have you any food and accommodation?').

While tourists clutter the mediaeval Devil's Bridge across the River Lune at Kirkby Lonsdale in old Westmorland, I lean on another bridge, less than a mile away, which was designed to carry pack-horses. So narrow is this bridge that a portly pedestrian would need to ford the stream. In the same county the Lune is crossed by a small bridge at a bend called the Crook of Lune, which you reach via a track underneath the sandstone arches of an obsolete railway viaduct. There indeed the busy world is hushed and the fever of life subsides, as though dispelled by the mountains. Many times I have leaned on that bridge, but only once did I meet anyone there, a farmer with his dog and six Herdwicks. In Scotland a bridge spans the stream beside a lane near the road from Blairgowrie to Braemar, a few miles south of the Spittal of Glenshee. Driving northward in sunshine, I followed the lane and soon reached the water, which felt icy despite the heat. Above it the mountains were streaked with snow. After five hours' driving I was weary; after half-an-hour's resting I was invigorated. If I ever pass that way again in hot weather I shall return to the bridge and the stream and the cuckoo calling from the foot of a white-capped ben.

It was during August that I first entered Otterburn, the Border ballad village in Northumberland. Having driven over the moor from Bellingham (they call it Bellinjam), I reached a little bridge across the Otter Burn, and there I rested, beguiled by the sparkling water. Ahead stood a handsome old building, formerly, a tweed mill and still a tweed shop, flanked by flowers. Before proceeding, I splashed my face and hands while the sun shone and the silence whispered. Only once have I failed to receive a refreshingly cool reception, and that was at Great Missenden in the Buckinghamshire Chilterns, where I found the Misbourne dried up because its water had been diverted to supply refugees from the London blitz. The course was a grass hollow, strewn with a few fag-ends and scraps of paper.

Some bridges are private, like the one above the moat that surrounds a friend's house in Warwickshire. Whenever I am a summer guest there I like to lean on the bridge, peering down at the swans and ducks, and stooping to touch the head of a young member of the family gliding by in a dinghy. Even during the hottest weather the shadows of the trees and the sunlight on the water seem to reduce the temperature. In the same county and at the home of another friend is a wooden bridge which I regard with special affection, for the following reason: this friend had often said that he would like to have a brook flowing through his garden, spanned by a bridge. Well, he eventually retired to Warwickshire, to a house whose garden does have a brook flowing through it, and in order to complete his wish he built a bridge there. It may be the smallest in Britain, perhaps in the world. I would set its length at eighteen inches and the width at a dozen. Nevertheless, it is undeniably a bridge whereon I am refreshed by the sibilant water and a border of grass and flowers.

8

Rubric

At this season a number of English villages celebrate a festival of things ancient and modern. Some of the celebrants are octogenarians; others are members of a Young Farmers club; all assemble to observe Lammas, which used to fall on the first day of August, but is now held on the first Sunday. A thousand years ago the festival was called *Hlafmaesse* or 'loaf of barley', a name that became Lamb-mass, a reference to the paschal-lamb. Although some people regard the observance as archaic, others value it as an expression of wonder and gratitude, a rubric or red-letter day in the countryman's calendar, expressing the belief of a Victorian poet, Norman Gale:

> God comes down in the rain,
> And the crop grows tall—
> This is the country faith,
> And the best of all.

The Roman Church long ago devised services to mark the high points of a farming year, but the services waned after the Reformation, and it was not until the 1940s that the English Church encouraged its clergy to revive them. One of the revivalists was Dr Bell, Bishop of Chichester, at whose invitation a Sussex parish priest, Canon Andrew Young—winner of the Queen's Gold Medal for Poetry—wrote a Lammas hymn that was printed in the BBC hymnal: 'Lord, by whose breath all souls and seeds are living . . .' A Sussex magazine pointed out that the purpose of a Lammas service is 'to offer the first fruit of the crops to God: and to offer Him the first food made in the village from these early crops . . .'. The compilers of the service kept an eye on the weather, stating the crop is 'an offering, irrespective of what the results have been, or are to be'. The same magazine explained that 'a sheaf of corn, and a loaf (made from the wheat that has just ripened) are

brought to church by members of the village and farming communities'. This sense of locality was emphasized by R. S. Hawker, a Victorian vicar of Morwenstow in Cornwall, who revived the Harvest Festival by announcing that the bread for Holy Communion would be baked from corn which had been reaped in Morwenstow.

Even the livestock used to take part in Lammastide, for on the first day of August they were set to graze on hayfields lately mown. In East Anglia this custom was called Lammas Shack (shack being a dialect word, meaning 'grain to be gleaned'). The Michaelmas Shack came later, when livestock were set to graze on stubble after the corn harvest. Both the spirit and the substance of Lammas have changed since machinery ousted men and horses from their work on the land. In Wiltshire last summer I visited a farm where two hundred acres of grain were being cut by three men and one machine. At six o'clock in the evening, when the last load had been carted, the men drove home, each in his own car. Neither they nor the farmer partook of a traditional harvest supper. Very different was the harvest of 1389 in a Suffolk parish when two hundred acres had been reaped by 520 men in two days. Food for the harvesters was prepared by a cook, a baker, and a brewer. The menu offered meat, herring, cheese, bread, butter, milk, ale. Candles to illuminate the meal were supplied by the lord of the manor. Such feasts are unlikely ever to recur, yet in deep country the old ways die hard. Only a few years ago I entered a cornfield near my house, following a path between the crop and a dry-stone wall. August burned so brightly that I sat down awhile, with the corn standing higher than my head. From time to time a breeze sidled among the stalks, which then uttered faint cracklings. Three days later, happening to pass the same field, I heard the clip-clop of hooves on the lane, and saw the farmer leading his shire-horse to harvest. Within five minutes the horse began to haul the reaper. The task was very much a family affair, with brother and sister and grandad to lend a hand. Knowing that I would be welcome, I returned at teatime and found the harvesters seated in the shade, awaiting the farmer's wife who soon arrived with tea, cakes, scones, and a pie. Reclining at ease, we did not envy the harvesters who toil all day on a combine, unable to hear the birds or to smell anything except oil. Progress often imposes heavy obligations.

At the end of the week I revisited the field and was greeted by an unexpected pleasure because the crops were stooked in the old style, each sheaf seeming to have been sculptured from amber stone. Above the sheaves, the Exmoor heights glowed with purple heather, and above the heather the sky outshone even the glossiest postcard. Aware that such scenes are almost unknown in England. I went home to fetch a camera; and whenever I give an illustrated talk about country life, that photograph of the sheaves evokes a gasp of astonishment; and whenever I explain that the photograph was taken only a few years ago, the astonishment verges on incredulity.

And now I am once more in the same field, surrounded by a similar crop under a similar sky. Whether the horse-reaper will appear I cannot say, but the birds are here, and so is the moorland heather. The same breeze causes the same faint cracklings among the sheaves. The same heights carve the same arcs. Peering above the corn, I see sheep in the combe far below; very lean they look, white and lately shorn. If I stood up and turned southward I would sight the Dartmoor mountains thirty miles away; and there, too, the combes and the foothills are ready to yield a Lammas offering. When I begin to make a few notes about the scene, my pencil and writing pad feel quite hot, and as I finish each sentence the sun seems to say that in such glorious weather nobody ought to do any work at all.

A Cool Reception

How pleasant it is when a sun-scorched walker sights a sparkling stream. During my own summer safaris I have thanked many waters for their beauty and refreshment. Two such slakings are especially memorable. The first occurred at Fighledean (local people call it File-dean) on the edge of Salisbury Plain, where I had been walking while, as Edward Thomas put it, 'Dry August burned.' Fortunately, I found a river in a secluded meadow, and there I swam, diving from the bole of a fallen tree. No towel was necessary. Sunlight sufficed. I sometimes regard that as the most enjoyable of all my total immersions. The second slaking occurred near Blickling Hall, Norfolk's stateliest mansion, where Anne Boleyn lived, in the years before she wore an uneasy crown. Again the month was August; again it burned; and again I found a stream, this time just wide enough to provide a cool bath. Once more the sun served as a towel.

Even if swimming is impossible, one may paddle. Something of the sort took place in Caithness when I was walking through the twenty miles of wilderness between Forsinard and Helms-

dale, under a sun so fierce that I wilted. However, the dog suddenly disappeared round a bend and presently returned, dripping like a sponge. Marooned in a land of peat, I supposed that he had entered a bog, but I was wrong; his keen ears had detected the tinkle of a brook. Sure enough, I soon found a miniature waterfall cascading down some rocks beside the lane. Having stooped to drink Gideon-fashion, I removed my socks and boots, allowing the icy water to ease the swollen ankles. Although I had walked all the morning without meeting anyone, and although I was to walk all the afternoon in the same solitude, the lack of company was compensated by several other streams *en route*, each one seeming to harmonize with Edmund Blunden's water music:

> Of all things young the brooks are not loved least,
> So sparking from their birth and dancing so;
> Their happy solitude has never ceased
> To call the wise to wander where they flow.

Do you happen to know the upper reaches of the Stour at Halford in Warwickshire? Seen from the grassy knoll above a lane that used to be gated, the stream resembles a silver thread whose loops may travel fifty yards in order to advance by a dozen. There, too, in water that glinted blue and gold, I enjoyed an amphibious respite from the high-summer heat. Do you know the Isis—Matthew Arnold's 'stripling Thames'—where it flows past Kelmscot in Oxfordshire, lapping the garden of William Morris's venerable home? Morris himself was so fond of the place that he confessed: 'As others love the race of man through their lover or their children, so I love the earth through this small space of it.' The Wylye in Wiltshire is another river which passes handsome architecture. W. H. Hudson described the buildings on the banks as 'among the principal charms of the Wylye—the sense of beautiful human things hidden from sight among the masses of foliage.'

At Holford, a hamlet in the Quantocks, the stream hurries downhill among woods. Without doubt it is one of several that enchanted the Wordsworths when they were staying at

Alfoxden: 'streams clear and pebbly,' Dorothy called them, 'as in Cumberland.' Izaak Walton knew the Dove at Milldale in Staffordshire (the banks climb to a wooded rampart). Sir Walter Scott knew Hermitage Water near Newcastleton in Roxburghshire (he set the Liddesdale scene in *Quentin Durward*). Delius knew the river at Brigg in Lincolnshire (I once found a leaky boat there, and punted it with my walking stick). R. D. Blackmore knew the Brayley at East Buckland in Devon (a serpent creeping through a ravine). Mary Queen of Scots knew the Nene at Fotheringhay in Northamptonshire (a meditation among level meadows).

Richard Jefferies knew the Barle at Simonsbath in Somerset ('it splashes,' he noticed, 'like boys bathing'). Emily Brönte knew the Worth near Haworth in Yorkshire (fed by becks from Keighley Moor). Michael Drayton knew the Eden in Westmorland ('My bright brook,' he called it). Gilbert White knew the stream at Cheriton in Hampshire (sidling past sedge). Robert Bridges knew a stream near Walmer in Kent ('clear and gentle'). Shelley knew the Thames at Great Marlow in Buckinghamshire (while boating there he composed part of 'The Revolt of Islam') Hugh Walpole knew the stream at Ashness Bridge in Cumbria (near there he set the home of Judith Paris). Wordsworth knew the Duddon in Lakeland (and to it he dedicated fourteen sonnets).

But a river in August needs no other commendation than its own cool rusticity. Indeed, a small stream in a sequestered valley may prove more rewarding than a great river beside noble buildings, for the stream's privacy is greater, and its music more intimate. If you do discover a stream by chance, the unexpectedness becomes a supererogation of refreshment. One of the streams at Meadle in Buckinghamshire is scarcely three feet wide, yet it offers a summer sparkle and a perennial *Nachtmusik* to the people through whose garden it flows.

From Cornwall to Caithness the summer months are slaked by famous rivers and by nameless brooks. The list is so long that no man will ever finish it. He can only compare notes with kindred spirits, trusting that each will find pleasure in the others' recollections.

Green Roads

Like a dark shadow on a vast sheepwalk, the green road crosses the Roxburghshire Cheviots. One of the neighbouring hills is called Bloodybush Edge, an echo from a moss-trooping past. On a bright summer morning, however, those Border feuds seem far off and long ago. Today the sheep graze safely, the birds sing blithely, the becks flow bluely. In such a place at such a time even the most phlegmatic wayfarer may experience Hazlitt's euphoria: 'Give me the clear blue sky over my head, and the green turf beneath my feet . . . I laugh, I run, I leap, I sing for joy.'

Many of our green roads were pioneered by prehistoric nomads driving their herds to new pastures, but this Roxburghshire road is neither very old nor very important, though farmers still use it when moving livestock over short distances. On most days of the year you can follow the road for several miles without seeing a human being; on the other days you may meet a shepherd going the rounds. When the flocks are rounded up for shearing and dipping, you may meet drovers on horseback, accompanied by dogs.

The green roads are not confined to remote or mountainous regions. They traverse a large area of Britain. Some of them, like the Berkshire Ridgeway, were first trodden by Celtic pedlars and pilgrims; others, like the Roman Dere Street from York to the Scottish border, were at one time paved, but are now either overgrown with grass or buried under a modern surface. Many green roads were trade routes, some of which became known as Salt Ways, like the route that led from the salt deposits in Cheshire. There were Sugar Ways, too, but the name is deceptive, being sour rather than sweet (the original version, *Scocera Weg*, meant Robbers Way). Some of the roads are relatively new, like the Pennine Way from Edale in Derbyshire to Kirk Yetholm in Roxburghshire, 250 miles of grass track, stony path, and country lane.

Until railways arrived, many green roads resounded to the bleating and bellowing of sheep and cattle, guided and goaded by mounted drovers *en route* to the nearest market or perhaps to a distant one. The livestock were usually penned overnight on a farmer's land at so much per head, whence the field-names of Farthing Close and Halfpenny Piece. John Clare set the scene during the early years of the nineteenth century:

> Scotch droves of beast, a little breed,
> In sweltered weary mood proceed,
> A patient race from Scottish hills
> To fatten by our pasture rills.

Although some of the drovers were tipsy and shifty, others possessed an intelligence and integrity which qualified them to act as messengers and agents. Scottish lairds and Welsh squires entrusted such men with large sums of money (the head drover for Sir Watkin Williams-Wyn once carried the equivalent of £50,000 to London). A Welsh drover, Benjamin Evans, became a dissenting minister. Six other Welsh drovers subscribed to Dr Johnson's dictionary. One or two founded their own banks, like The Black Sheep Bank or *Banc y Dafad Ddu* at Aberystwyth. Every drover earned good wages and received a bonus if his charges arrived safely.

Green roads may be found in unlikely places, as at Royston in Hertfordshire, where the main road follows the course of a prehistoric track, the Icknield Way, from Cambridgeshire to the west country. Just beyond Royston the modern road turns north-west while the ancient one continues as a grass track. A comparable divergence occurs on yet another modern road that follows the course of an old one, the Roman Fosse Way between Lincoln and the Devon coast near Seaton. Not far from Cirencester, at a wooded dell called Jackaments Bottom, the modern route veers away while the Roman road continues as a green track on which you can walk for several hours, touching only the tip of a hamlet at Easton Grey, a Roman–British settlement beside a stream. It is difficult to believe that this unfrequented track was once a paved highway, patrolled by Roman soldiers, followed by Celtic peasants and by government officials. I have walked, too, on a green road which now covers the Roman one through Northumberland to Trimontium or the Eildon Hills near Sir Walter Scott's Abbotsford in Selkirkshire. This road crosses some of the wildest scenery in the border country. Segments of green road exist on yet another Roman route, the Peddars or Pedlars Way from Ixworth in Suffolk to Holme-next-the-Sea in Norfolk. A mile or more beyond Castle Acre, at a spot called Shepherds Bush, the metalled lane leads to Great Massingham while the Peddars Way becomes a green road through pasture and corn. This really was a Robbers Way, used by smugglers as a route from the coast. James Woodforde's diary admitted that contraband was left at his Norfolk parsonage: 'Andrews the smuggler brought me this night about 11 o'clock a bag of Hysop Tea . . . He frightened us a little by whistling under the Parlour Window just as we were going to bed. I paid him for the tea at 10/6 per Pd.'

England in Woodforde's day was a green land, able to raise much food, and scarcely soiled by industry. England in our own day is over-populated, infested with traffic, harried by aircraft, and not beautified by industry. As a result, more and more townsfolk are seeking an escape from monotonous employment in a dreary environment. The green roads offer just such a refuge. On them you can walk as it were out of the frying pan into the fresh air, and at the end of the seventh mile, or perhaps at the beginning of the second, you may meet a shepherd and his dog or a lover and his lass, to whom wars and strikes are not of paramount importance. Some of those roads will carry you over the hills and far away from human habitations; others will carry you to the edge of hamlets and villages and small towns. In more senses than one the green roads lead to the heart of things.

Old Omniscience

The octogenarian Canon and the middle-aged Dr Keys are in many ways so unlike that their friendship is a merging of contraries. The Canon, Sir Reginald, achieved a classical fellowship at Oxford, but when his wife and son died in childbirth he took Holy Orders and became parson of his ancestral parish, eventually inheriting the title and estate from his elder brother. Dr Keys, on the other hand (known among friends as Caius), achieved a classical fellowship at Cambridge, where the undergraduates call him Old Omniscience, partly because he looks nearly as venerable as his own father and partly because he is voluble and erudite. Bound by a bond of mutual scholarship, Dr Keys often visits the Canon's manor house in the north country, arriving as a rule either before or after the appointed date, so that the Canon has been heard to say: 'Dear Caius will be arriving on Monday, or Tuesday, or Wednesday.' This neglect of the calendar is commonly attributed to the Doctor's preoccupation with the Messianic nuances of what he calls 'That fourth Eclogue'.

When the two men do meet, their clothes emphasize another difference, because on informal occasions the Canon wears a tweed jacket and a corduroy cap, whereas the Doctor always wears clerical black and no headgear at all (this causes a breeze to uplift his few strands of grey hair, which then resemble attenuated wings). As the visitor's suitcase is filled almost entirely with books, the Canon's housekeeper, Mrs Loveday, provides shaving tackle, clean underwear, and a dressing-gown.

At their first encounter with Dr Keys the villagers were baffled, never before having seen or heard anyone like him. When the postman remarked that the days were drawing in, the Doctor murmured a few words of Latin which caused the postman to ask his neighbours whether anyone in the district knew a young chap called Pliny. The Canon's shepherd expressed a general verdict: 'To luke at him thou'd think a feather would bowl him over, but owd Garth Thwaite saw him on't fell at cock-crow. Nimble as an 'Erdwick, Garth said, and dressed like he were going to a funeral.'

The Doctor usually enjoys one session at the Blacksmiths Arms, during which time the listeners sit spellbound, signalling rather than calling for another pint. 'Farming and machines?' the Doctor says. 'My dear fellow, we are all of us machines. The Canon happens to be the kind of machine which believes that machinery contains a Deus or benevolent designer. I happen to be the kind of machine which believes . . . but there's no need of a Hegelian dialectic.' The company relaxes when the Oracle changes his tune. 'He sold 'em the most lifelike dummy I've ever seen. Then he raced thirty glorious yards on the edge of the line and finally made a triumphant touch-down between the posts. Of course, we had to rusticate him for sheer ignorance, but we arranged for him to come up in time for the Varsity match.' On most evenings, however, the two friends retire to the Canon's library, there to smoke several peaceful pipes while chewing the cud of classical problems, ancient as well as modern, thereby deserving Edmund Blunden's praise:

> But here at least a classic education
> Was honoured yet, and sound examination
> Worshipped in form, and should be, evermore.

Since the Doctor simultaneously talks and eats throughout every meal, the maid-servant has been instructed to remove his plate without impeding his peroration. Afterwards, when asked to give an opinion of the game pie, he is apt to say:'Oh, is that what we had?' Only the Canon and the cook know of the morning when the Doctor, having eaten a hearty breakfast at 6.45 a.m. went for a five-mile walk and then joined his host for a second hearty breakfast at 9 a.m.

On the final evening of the Doctor's latest visit the Canon gave a small dinner party, the guests being skilfully mixed to include a former high sheriff, an MFH, a Jesuit who spoke Latin, and the widow of a colonial governor, lately converted to Buddhism. The Doctor himself was in fine form and managed to finish his soup before the widow had unfolded her napkin. During the meal he diagnosed some of the rarer diseases among foxes and then exposed the perils of what he called disproportional misrepresentation. When coffee was served he cited the Germanic origins of the lead pencil trade at Keswick, Luther's fondness for hunting, the Michelson-

Morley zero, the effects of the Defenestration of Prague, Schubert's alleged cribbing from Beethoven, and the speed at which Lord Cardigan led the charge of the Light Brigade: 'Fourteen miles an hour, my dear Sir, a steady canter. Army regulations, in fact. No headlong galloping.' With a glance at the Jesuit he murmured 'Solus Deus salus'.

As with the guest's arrival, so with his departure, for they both cause the Canon to hedge his bets when informing the housekeeper: 'Dr Keys will be leaving on Thursday, or Friday, or Saturday.' While the guest himself is saying goodbye, the housekeeper searches his bedroom and is not surprised to discover various small items—socks, spectacles, suspenders—which she hurriedly conveys to the waiting taxi-cab. During his first visit the Doctor left behind an item so important that the Canon now provides a small plastic box bearing the word *Dentes*. Schooled by experience, the taxi-driver pauses before switching on the engine, lest the Doctor or someone else suddenly remembers a book that was left in the WC, or a pocket-knife that fell under the billiard-table.

Finally, as the cab disappears down the drive, the Canon turns to his housekeeper, saying: 'Well, Mrs Loveday, it has, as usual, been an experience.'

Over the Counter

A post office may not be so popular as a pub, but it is a far more important feature of country life. Risking a generalization, I would say that the heydays of the village post office occurred toward the end of the nineteenth century, when telephones were rare, radio was unknown, and an increasing number of farmfolk wrote letters, and sometimes sent telegrams, to their relatives and friends. Flora Thompson's *Lark Rise to Candleford* described the postmistress at an Oxfordshire village, a kindly and competent Victorian spinster, 'whose commanding air gave her what was then known as "presence."' All sorts and conditions of customers called at the post office, and in summertime they combined the business of posting with the pleasure of promenading: 'Instead of rushing in a crowd to post at the last minute,' Miss Thompson wrote, 'they would stroll over the green in the afternoon and stay for a chat.'

Their heirs and successors still do stay for a chat, and I doubt that the topics of conversation have greatly changed since Miss Thompson's squire received his letters in a special satchel. On most days I am likely to hear someone tell the Devon postmistress: 'This yere's by hair mail, midear. 'Tis for my daughter in Australia. Her's just presented us with a grandson.' In less cheerful mood a shepherd will say: 'He suffers something terrible, poor soul. I keep telling 'en . . . if only 'ee'd see the doctor. But no, he's frightened they'd send 'en to a tri-siatric ward.' Arriving to collect his pension, a pillar of the nonconformist chapel mutters: 'They say the new minister's going to play his banjo after the sermon, but *I* say I'm hanged if I'll be there to hear 'en.' While renewing her television licence, a housewife complains about favouritism in high places: ''Tis the same every year. Other folks do the cooking for the fête, but 'tis her always gets the creeit.' I once heard a Westmorland postmaster answer back: 'Thee mun take thy complaint where it belongs. If a letter is addressed to Kendal, like thine was, then nobbut a fool would expect it to turn up at Kirkby Stephen.'

My own nearest post office is a very small room in a rather small house at a diminutive village two miles away; an office so secluded that strangers have been known to pass without seeing it. Even smaller is the post office at Winsford in Somerset, wedged between two houses facing Ernest Bevin's birthplace across the street. Since many rural post offices are picturesque, it would be absurd to cite one above the rest. However, some of them have, as we say, stuck in my memory, like the thatched office at Great Tew in Oxfordshire, a cottage which Viscount Falkland knew three centuries ago, when his manor house became famous as a meeting place for scholars and poets (Ben Jonson was among the latter). Unless my memory has played tricks, there used to be a thatched post office at Honington, a shopless and publess village near

Shipston-on-Stour in Warwickshire. There was certainly a post office at Penuwch, not a great way from Lampeter in Wales. The place was a tin shack. When I asked for a letter card the postmistress searched all the drawers and shelves and then retired to an inner compartment, staying there so long that I wondered whether she had been taken ill. Emerging at last, she said: 'Letter card, was it? We did have one, but I seem to have lost it.'

Business is not always brisk at John o'Groats in Caithness, the most northerly settlement on the British mainland. When I first arrived there, during March, the postmaster was surprised to see a visitor so early in the year. 'But,' he assured me, 'it's very different during the summer. Thousands of people come here, all wanting to send a card bearing our postmark. Each card must be marked by hand, and I often need my wife to help with the mountain of mail.' Have you seen the post office at Arley, a village of red-brick cottages on a cliff above the River Severn near Bridgnorth? At one of those cottages the post office-cum-stores combines modern efficiency with old-fashioned friendliness. I was similarly impressed by the post office-cum-stores at Shipton Gorge, a village near Bridport in Dorset. There the General comes to collect his daily newspaper, waiting patiently while a child decides how to invest a small coin ('No, I've changed my mind. Gimme the pepper-mint instead'). At the post office on Holy Island the postmistress proudly told me: 'I think I can say our family has kept the post office ever since there was a Holy Island.'

Have you seen the post office-cum-stores at Great Hampden in the Buckinghamshire Chilterns, a brick-and-flint cottage overlooking the green, where private enterprise co-exists amicably with a State monopoly? In that snug retreat, many years ago, I heard the blacksmith say: 'You wouldn't remember old Reuben, but I do. He went into the Great Missenden post office one day, 'cause his nephew worked as a telegram boy there, and on that day that boy was seventeen years old, so Reub sent hisself a telegram so's the boy could deliver it in time for a cup of tea and a slice of birthday cake.' At Ballinger, a village in the same county, the post office-cum stores was kept by Miss Gray, a delightful and cultivated woman. Even during the 1950s the shop was lit by an oil lamp suspended from the ceiling, and whenever I called there my dog received a biscuit or some other titbit.

In Flora Thompson's day the cottagers needed to watch every penny. In our own day you may hear a young garage mechanic say: 'Send 'en express, Missus. I've changed my plans. Going to Spain, not Majorca. If this yere arrives before the end o' the month I'll get a reduction, so the trip won't cost me much more than a couple of hundred quid.'

9

Equinox

Every year we know that it will strike. Every year it does strike, and every year we are taken aback. Some people call it the first of the equinoctial gales, which is a misnomer because an equinox cannot bring more than one gale. Equinoxes (Latin *aequus* meaning equal) occur twice a year, during the second half of March and September, when the length of the day equals the length of the night. By whatever name and at whatever date, the first autumnal gale is usually wilder than a summer one and always more sombre since it heralds the dark months. The effects of such gales seem especially severe when they succeed a spell of calm weather. Lulled by September's halcyon warmth, we pretend that summer is still alive . . . a delusion fostered by gnats circling in a shaft of sunshine which itself makes the grass look greener than it did in August. Bees abound, bumbling among hollyhocks and honeysuckle. Sometimes a bee disappears into a snapdragon, which then droops and drones. Admittedly the brown leaves confound our summer daydream, but by glancing above them (at a cloudless sky) and then below them (at a flower-filled border) we can forget that in a few weeks' time the clocks must be put back. Eventually, however, the daydream is dispersed when a gale strikes hard:

> And in one mighty stream, invisible,
> Immense, the whole excited atmosphere
> Impetuous rushes o'er the sounding world . . .

To modern ears James Thomson's seasonal set piece may seem orotund, yet it is at least comprehensible at a first reading. People who live among mountains or moorlands will allow that Thomson said what he meant and thereby shared what he saw:

> Red from the hills, innumerable streams
> Tumultuous roar . . .

During a wet autumn in northern districts, where the corn may stand until October, farmers will agree that Thomson evoked their own rain-swept plight:

> . . . all that the winds had spared
> In one wild moment ruined, and big hopes
> And well-earned treasures of the painful years.

On the morning after a September gale the land appears to have aged overnight. Some of the trees show bald patches, and their fallen leaves are slotted into dry-stone walls, or slapped against windows, or glued to gutters. Hurled twenty yards by the wind, the last rose of summer floats like a lily on the pond. Hidden since Easter, bird-nests are brief memorials to arduous ingenuity. Ripped from the roof of a shed, two strips of corrugated metal lie in the middle of the lane, indented by a passing tractor. Flowerbeds resemble disintegrating rainbows. Emily Brönte, that fearless spirit, welcomed the autumn. 'Every leaf,' she said, 'speaks bliss to me,/Fluttering from the autumn tree.' Less intrepid spirits share W. H. Davies's gloom:

> Is this old Autumn standing here,
> Where wind-blown fruits decay;
> Dressed up in limp, bedraggled flowers
> That Summer cast away?

In coastal regions the gale utters an even sterner warning. If you have lived in a small boat on salt-water during September you will have heard that warning, and felt it, too.

Though you are anchored in a creek, the wind and waves will track you down, for creeks may serve as funnels which intensify the uproar. Crockery clatters in the locker. A tin of condensed milk capsizes, oozing through butter and a dish of sardines. Slung from the cabin door, an oilskin sways like a filleted ghost. Sea-boots slither across the deck, dizzy as Rimbaud's *bateau ivre*. Bilges gurgle, and if the clinkers hull is elderly you go on deck, pelted and buffeted, to work the pump. When the light fails, you throw out a second anchor. All night the boat tugs at her chain while halyards rattle and the dinghy dives.

Next morning, proceeding towards the open sea, you meet breakers that send their spume above the cabin roof. The coast wears a necklace woven by winds that have scoured flotsam and jetsam from the harbour's nooks and crannies. Baulks of timber appear, surging through a Sargasso of scum, ropes, tins, weeds, paper. Yesterday you were cruising three miles offshore; today you put back because the propeller is racing. Prodded by pooping wind and water, you notice that several boats have broken loose and are either beached or drifting in midstream. One of them—a sizeable cabin cruiser—has rammed her bowsprit into a clump of trees on the bank; another has lost her tarpaulin, which now floats into the harbour, like a strange species of seaweed. At a farm overlooking the ferry, a Vacancies sign has been tilted upside-down, and six slates are missing from the roof. Bales of clifftop corn have been swept onto the beach, together with skeins of twine and a tin of kerosine.

The ferry itself arrives late, after a rough passage across the bay, during which the helmsman took evasive action when he sighted a flotilla of vagrant lobster pots. Bobbing at her mooring, the lifeboat looks smaller than ever, and even more necessary. The coxswain's car stands near his cottage, just in case. At the quayside Mariners Arms the stone walls shudder while smoke from the hearth either fumigates the tap room or is flattened parallel with the roof. Waves break over the jetty, seething and stinging. A man is chasing his cap. In short—to misquote a famous weather bulletin—'Summer is icumen out'.

The Same Yet Different

Seen from outside, the place looks much as it did a century ago. The roof is still thatched, and sparrows still twitter among the eaves. The horse-trough and the mounting block are there, and above them the sign, George and Dragon; but when you enter, some of the changes are garish as the carpet that now hides the bare-board floor. Arriving after many years' absence, an elderly villager would be dazzled by the harsh lighting that has replaced the mellow oil lamps. Remembering the wooden benches and a deal table, he would dislike the cheap chairs and red-topped stools. When he glanced up, however, he would recognize the print of Queen Victoria at her diamond jubilee, flanked by a portrait of the present Queen and by a photograph of the landlord as a leading seaman in 1950.

The hearth remains unchanged, and so does the fire-basket, big enough to take logs four feet long. In front of it a grizzled sheepdog sleeps alongside a tabby cat. Another old friend is the country-made grandfather clock, its dial inscribed Jos. Jones 1799. The counter, too, is recognizable, indented by many coins, tankards, and cigarette ends; but several other agreeable features—the tinkling embers, the twittering sparrows, the ticking clock—all are drowned by canned cacophony from a loudspeaker above the mantelshelf. The space formerly occupied by a spittoon has been taken over by a machine whose flashing lights and crude pictures invite the customer to enrich the men who manufacture such contraptions. Few customers arrive on a bicycle, and none at all on a horse. The car park behind the vegetable patch is full on Saturday nights. Nevertheless, a ploughman still plods his thirsty way from an outlying cottage, following a footpath through Castle Wood and then a lane past the old water-mill. The time of his arrival is so punctual that some people say he consults his watch before entering.

Since a market town lies less than six miles away, many of the younger villagers prefer to drive there, if only because The Bull has more gambling machines and a louder loudspeaker. Unless

the rain is very heavy, or the roads icy, the tap room at the George and Dragon always contains several customers who have been young and now are old. Like their fathers' fathers, they discuss the weather, the crops, their own infirmities, and the latest burial. 'I see from the *Chronicle*', says Albert, 'poor old Sam Varney has gone at last. He'd a bad time of it towards the end.'

'And yet,' says Percy, 'I can remember when Sam thought nothing of walking here from his place at Fiveways. Must ha' been eight mile, there and back. And whenever Sam took too much, the landlord . . . Stoker Bill we called him 'cause he'd been a sailor . . . Bill would tell Sam to go home. But old Sam would walk another four mile to The Wheatsheaf.'

'But he didn't always get there,' Albert replies. 'More than once his Dad and me went out to look for him. Sometimes we'd find him asleep in Reuben's barn. And that night . . . when was it? He'd come home on leave, I remember . . . anyway, there was a blizzard raging, so three of us went to search for him. Lucky to be alive, were Sam. He'd fallen into Reub's sheep dip and broken his ankle. "Merry Christmas, Sam," I said, though 'twas only Guy Fawkes night. "Christmas already?" he said, "In that case it's too bloody white for *my* liking." ' Turning in his chair, Harry adds a postscript: 'All that ended when he married Lucy. Made him sign the pledge, Lucy did. He once said to me, "Harry, I'm a changed man, and there's times I wish I wasn't." '

The veterans assess past and present as impartially as they can, and their verdict is unanimous: 'I reckon things were about all right in the 1950s, but nowadays too much of 'em is all wrong.' Younger men, on the other hand, praise the new machines and also holidays with pay: 'You won't catch me working for five quid a week.'

'Five quid?' says Albert 'I raised three kids on 30 bob.'

'But . . .'

'But *you've* spent more than that since you got here an hour ago.'

One recent innovation the veterans disapprove vehemently . . . the women and young girls who on Saturday night almost outnumber the men. As Albert put it: 'If old Reuben could see 'em, I don't know what he'd do, but I know very well what he'd say. "Babylon," that's what he'd say. In fact, I fancy he'd shout it. A great Baptist, old Reub were.'

A sunny summer morning is a good time to visit the George and Dragon, when the windows are wide open, and some of the veterans sit on a bench outside. Even better, perhaps, is a winter night, shortly after opening time, when the tap room is still spared the loudspeaker, and most of the company are either middle-aged or old. At such moments you feel that Time has not wholly outdated Edmund Blunden's village inn:

> Round all the nooks and corners goes
> The evening talk, in this old inn;
> The darkening room by use well knows
> Each thread of life that these upspin.

By the Fire

The evening was so wet and misty that walking became a penance rather than a pleasure. After half an hour, therefore, I returned home and was greeted by firelight flickering from the window. Having groomed the damp dog, I lit a pipe, threw another log on the fire, and pulled my chair close to the glow. There is nothing to rival a wood fire on an open hearth or even in a stove with the doors open. Central heating may prove more pervasive; electricity exudes less dirt; coal emits more heat; but well-seasoned logs are still a countryman's favourite toes-toaster, and if the logs are cherry or apple the nose also will benefit, inhaling an aromatic aura from the flames.

Do you remember those dark days a year ago when—either on our own land or with permission on someone else's—we collected the fuel which warms this year's dark days? Though the task may have seemed tedious at the time, are we not reaping a radiant harvest from our labours? Do we not gaze complacently at the twigs in the wood shed, dry and inflammable, the foundation of our fire; then at the wrist-thick logs, likewise dry, which answer instantly to the twigs; and finally at the larger logs, the slow burners, each one topped and tailed so that it fits neatly into the hearth? I sometimes enter the wood shed solely in order to admire its contents, rather as a miser counts his money, though my own treasury will be spent, not hoarded.

I have sat beside some splendid fires. The most spacious was at a friend's moated house, where, if they wish, guests can sit in the hearth itself, facing one another across the flames. Between September and March this vast cavern is never allowed to grow cold, for the logs are laid on a mound of Alp-like ash. Each morning, therefore, one puff from the bellows creates a spark which kindles the new fuel. Only a few miles from my home, a lonely inn contains a hearth big enough to burn logs four feet long. Rescued from a snowdrift, or half-drowned by rain, lambs have revived at this hearth, bottle-fed with warm milk before returning to the ewes. When hounds meet at the inn, the scarlet coats vie with the crackling flames, and more than one sportsman, who had intended to follow on foot, stays behind, watching the rain while sipping his ale.

Even a cheerless room responds to firelight. I remember being marooned by dense fog which forced me to seek accommodation at a small country hotel. Arriving too late for dinner and too early for bed, I was shown into a cold and dreary residents' lounge containing a few pieces of shoddy furniture; but when the landlord lit a fire the room was transformed within a couple of minutes. The ash-tray—it resembled an old-fashioned dentist's spittoon—gleamed like an iridescent incense-burner. The Brummagem murals—toasting forks and horse bridles—could have passed as burnished copper. Even the carpet lost some of its mauveness. When a girl arrived with a plate of egg and chips, she exclaimed: 'What a difference a fire makes!'

In more ways than one a fire out of doors has saved countless lives. Our prehistoric ancestors lit fires at the entrances to their caves, hoping to deter wolves and other carnivorous marauders. A portable stove, too, is still useful. Robert Louis Stevenson, for example, spent a night among the pine forests of the Cevennes, waking to a chilly dawn and the task of preparing a hot drink. In gratitude for that agreeable experience, he wrote: 'It pleased me, in a half-laughing way, to leave pieces of money on the turf as I went along, trusting they would not fall to some rich and churlish drover.' Another writer, George Borrow often basked beside a gipsies' fire, warming himself against the wind on the heath. Not long ago I saw several gipsies sitting round a fire near Whichford in Warwickshire. While their horses grazed the verge, the nomads cooked supper outside the caravan. For most people, however, a fire is primarily an indoor companion, though not necessarily a wood burner.

At John o'Groats I once met the Houston family, who then owned one of the two Scottish water-mills that still earned a living. The son stacked some peat in the boot of my car, and I celebrated several Christmas Eves by burning a piece, the scent whereof carried me northward over the miles and years. Peat, by the way, is not merely a tepid comforter, acrid and smouldering; on the contrary, peat that has been properlv cut and dried gives ample heat and cheerful flames. Nevertheless, wood remains the most popular domestic fuel among country-folk who have easy access to it. Some households praise ash as a quick burner; some prefer oak as a slow burner; some choose beech as a reliable all-rounder. Seasoned elm is not to be despised, but elder scarcely justifies the labour of felling.

My own shed contains a pile of wood for special occasions. Each log has been seasoned for at least a year, and all were chosen for a particular merit . . . apple and cherry because of their fragrance, holly because of its vivid flame, oak (from a seventeeth-century rafter) because of its intense heat. This evening, to mark a friend's birthday, I am burning apple. The scent of it, curling above the chimney, reached us while we were still fifty yards from the house.

Coast and Country

It was with some anxiety that I approached a region notorious for religious and political strife. Anxiety, however, was tinged with sadness because both sides of the divide contained men whose means were peaceable and whose ends were reasonable. So there I stood, in a pastoral stillness which might at any moment be shattered by feuds that were old four hundred years ago, when the poet Spenser spoke from his own

experience as secretary to Lord Grey of Wilton, Lord-Deputy in Ireland: 'It is the fatal destiny of Ireland that no purposes whatever which are meant for her good will prosper . . .'

Having reached the danger zone, I saw something which I shall not easily forget. In the middle of a village street two men were talking cordially, each with an arm on the other's shoulder. Of the men's identity there could be no doubt, for their attire showed that one of them was a Roman priest and that the other was a Protestant minister. I drove on, minding my own business, which was to reach Ulster and the Mountains of Mourne; but the sight of these two men, arm-linked and amicable, reminded me that there are moments when we feel torn between hope and despair, uncertain whether to retreat or whether to return once more to an apparently irreparable breach.

Just south of the Border I ran into an autumnal mist and very nearly into a vagabond who was strolling in the middle of the highway. While taking evasive action, I came uncomfortably close to a pony and trap that were on the wrong side of the road. During the brief and blurred encounter the trapman called: 'Top o' the morning to you! The sun is on his way.' Having halted in order to regain my bearings, I was able to overhear the trapman's misty encounter with the middle-of-the-roader. 'If I didn't know you,' he shouted, 'I'd say you was drunk. But I do know you, which is another way o'stating that you never get drunk till teatime. At present it's not yet midday, so will you kindly re-orientate yourself before the police arrest you red-handed for being Patrick Murphy.'

Following a car-free route north of the Border, I joined the lane that crosses the seaward side of the Mourne Mountains. Frustrated by the mist, I felt inclined to turn back, but was encouraged when the sun took the words from the trapman's mouth. First came a rift, then a series of rifts, and then a rolling-back of the curtain to reveal a sea-blue sky. Once more I halted, this time to scan the mountains, a gaunt and rocky range, whose inmost tracts are accessible only to walkers and horsemen. The land on either side of the lane was littered with boulders, rather as though an earthquake had scattered innumerable stone walls. Sheep were so sparse that I looked twice lest I had mistaken them for rocks. No building was visible; not even a bield. On my left the wilderness climbed to distant summits; on my right it descended towards the sea, but so gradually that the coast remained hidden. Despite the solitude, two voices echoed in my ears. The first, which I had heard in Belfast, said: 'We'll never submit to British rule.' The second, which I had heard on board ship, said: 'If a political party loses an election in England, that's that. But if a political party loses an election in Ulster, that's not that, because the losers expect to join the winners in forming a government.'

The peace of the mountains was so pervasive that I soon

drove on, descending deviously until the sea appeared as well as the land, each shining in sunlight, a triptych of blue and green and grey, dappled with white blobs which might have been sheep, or rocks, or crofts. After a few miles a croft did appear, but its isolation was heightened rather than diminished by the sight of a second croft. As though addressing the sheep, I said:

> Here men and mountain dwell as one,
> Remembering the great deeds done
> In this high land where Kings once sat
> Enthroned as on Mount Ararat.

Presently I sighted a dozen fishing boats offshore, some with blue sails, some with brown, and some bare-masted while their engines churned a milky wake. Finally, the roofs of Kilkeel rose up, a small yet thriving harbour whose inhabitants are poised between the mountains and the sea, drawing sustenance from both.

On reaching England I recounted some of my experiences to the hotel porter, who told me that he was born in County Mayo, but had spent forty years in Ulster. I got the impression that his remarks applied to whatever was laudable on both sides of the Border. 'I'd gladly give all my electricity bills', he declared, 'in exchange for a whiff o' the peat, and all the toxic tins in exchange for a taste o' the gammon that hung like manna from the rafters. It was a blessed land, I'm thinking, and myself born at a blessed time despite the troubles. Never a car there was to bother my boyhood, unless maybe a gallivanting Englishman punctured his progress to Purgatory. The priest rode bareback on a borrowed donkey, so he did, with his toes trailing the dust. And if you'd just lost your shirt at the races, or was getting out o' the way o' the wife's tongue, sure the priest would say, "Step inside a minute. I've a drop o' something will rinse away the old Adam, and ease the pain o' your marital rib."'

The exile sighed. 'There's no place like Ireland. I'd be after going there myself were it not for the length o' my false teeth.' Clasping the silver coin which I slipped into his hand, the man from Mayo said: 'It's a darlin' country, so it is, and the people are the salt o' the earth when they've a mind to be sweet.'

Sleeping Rough

During a pre-breakfast stroll in the Sussex parish of Whatlington I stumbled on, though not actually against, a sleeping man whose grey stubble and dirty raincoat suggested that he was one of those vagabonds whom it is now fashionable to describe as under-privileged. However, his loud snores and bloated features led me to think that on the previous night he had been privileged to get drunk. Returning via the same path five minutes later, I found that the man had gone, leaving behind some crumbs and an empty cigarette packet. Although I pitied his state of mind, and did not envy his itchy body, I remembered that to sleep in the open air can be a pleasant experience, enabling one to escape from what Robert Louis Stevenson called 'the Bastille of civilization'.

In order to forestall decriers of the British climate, I admit that an alfresco sleep is not always restful. I once spent the night in a tent among the Buckinghamshire beech woods, trusting that May would live up to its merry sobriquet. To begin with, all went well. Serenaded by a fox and an owl, I soon feel asleep, but awoke shortly before midnight, probably because of the cold. Shortly after midnight the first snowflakes fell, causing the tent to glisten like an igloo. The next few hours were passed in a shivering stupor, neither wide awake nor fast asleep; and when at last the dawn chorus uttered a reveille more resonant than John Peel's hunting horn I would gladly have exchanged a damp tent in the woods for a dry dungeon in the Bastille. Despite the cynics, however, our warm months are not always cold. Besides, if an outdoor sleeper has already spent sixteen hours in the fresh air he is well on the way to de la Mare's Land of Nod.

> Softly along the road of evening,
> In a twilight dim with rose . . .

Through the twilight one bird—usually a blackbird or a thrush—sings solo to the setting sun. Rooks can become a nuisance, yet they, too, eventually pipe down, leaving the world to silence, or so it seems until a sheep bleats, or a dog barks, or a belfry strikes ten sonorous notes. If you are sleeping in a wood you will probably hear insects and rodents rustling the fallen leaves; soothing sounds and unlikely to presage harm. Livestock, by contrast, are not welcome, and for that reason you should set your tent or sleeping bag in a place that cattle and sheep cannot reach. When a cow plonks its feet or its nostrils within a yard of your head, it is difficult to believe that the creature feels more apprehensive than yourself. Avoid also ants, especially the species called, I think, *lugubris*; the ill-effects of its bite are in considerably more than inverse proportion to the smallness of its body.

Bedouins are not the only people who detect a pre-dawn or indefinable stirring before the sun has risen. Myself, I lack such perceptive antennae, but I do recall a Cornish night spent on the deck of my boat, anchored a short distance from the lighthouse at St Anthony-in-Roseland. A local sailor had assured me that, given propitious weather, the fish were sure to be found there. 'Look for the gulls,' he said, 'because under them you'll find whitebait. And under the whitebait you'll find bass.' Well, the afternoon was unsettled, but toward evening the sky cleared, the barometer rose, and the BBC predicted a glorious June dawn. Sure enough, we netted so many bass that at midnight the deck resembled a fishermonger's slab. My companions having rowed ashore, I slept in the open air, hearing only an occasional swish when the water sidled against the hull. Overhead, the stars confirmed the truth of Thomas Hardy's saying: 'Astronomy is peculiarly adapted to remedy a little and narrow spirit . . .'

Soon after sunrise the throb of a Customs launch woke me up. At about six o'clock I dropped anchor in the Percuil River, flanked by wooded hills, wherefrom two cuckoos repetitively recited their own name. By the time I had breakfasted, polished the brightwork, pumped the bilges, and taken a salt-water bath, the thermometer crept close to seventy degrees Fahrenheit. Outward bound for the oyster beds, a boatman called: 'You'm going to be frizzled afore dinnertime.'

Such a wide awake dawn, following such a fast asleep night, seems as it were to gild the beauty of an English summer day, when the sun shines high and hot from a cloudless sky, and a breeze tempers the sting, and every meadow and all the hills wear a new-laundered livery of green, trimmed with bluebells that chime silently, like the wavelets of a painted ocean. Then indeed we are granted a daylong parabola of scent and colour and sound, rising ecstatically from dawn's dim chorus, climbing leisurely to fervid noon, slanting serenely to a late thrush and a rose-red aura in the west. There are not many such days in each year; but when they come and while they last, all save the heaviest heart leaps up to greet them, and even the heaviest may lean on them, sharing its burden.

10

Corner-Stones of England

Not many years ago the sale of a country house caused quite a stir. Villagers discussed (and sometimes invented) reasons for the change of ownership. Today, by contrast, such sales are so common that even in deep country a house may change hands several times within a dozen years. This frequent buying and selling is one result of the reduction in the number of farm-hands, gamekeepers, blacksmiths, wheelwrights, millers, domestic servants, and all those others whom Gilbert White defined as 'stationary men', living and dying in their native county and perhaps in their native parish. Very different are the householders whose livelihood now takes them to a new district every few years. It is this compulsory mobility, rather than a radical change in human nature, which makes it difficult for some people to experience a love of home . . . not simply of a temporary house and garden, but of an orchard where they played as a child, near a lane where they lingered as a lover, beside a stream where they rested as a veteran.

Only during the past half century has that kind of allegiance become exceptional, and when they encounter it, many townsfolk dismiss it as sentimental. Accustomed to travelling far and fast and frequently, they find it almost impossible to believe that their grandparents preferred a less unsettled existence. Edmund Blunden, for example, acknowledged his debt to the people and places of his Kentish childhood; from the stress of later life, he said: 'I turned to you, I never turned in vain.' Another soldier-poet Wilfred Gibson, looked to Northumberland:

Just to see the rain
Sweep over Yeavering Bell
Once again.

Mary Webb spent her life in Shropshire, 'a county', she claimed, 'where the dignity and beauty of ancient things lingers long, and I was fortunate in being born and brought up in its magical atmosphere'. John Clare, on the other hand, lapsed into psychosis when he was forced to quit his native Northamptonshire:

I've left my own old home of homes,
Green fields and every pleasant place;
The summer like a stranger comes,
I pass, and hardly know her face.

William Morris saw in his Thames-side house at Kelmscot a sufficient *raison d'être*: 'As others love the race of men through their lover or their children, so I love the earth through this small space of it.' In later life Wilfred Scawen Blunt clung to his Sussex inheritance:

I covet not a wider range
Than these dear manors give;
I take my pleasures without change,
And as I lived I live.

'Stronger than a man . . . her nature stood alone.' Such was Charlotte Brönte's opinion of her sister Emily; yet even that indomitable woman wilted when she left her father's Yorkshire parsonage to serve as a governess on the Continent: 'Day by day', Charlotte recalled, 'I watched her sinking, a captive of captivity. Every morning when she awoke the vision of home and the moors rushed on her, and darkened and saddened the day . . . I felt in my heart that she would die, if she did not go home . . .' Andrew Crosse, the Victorian scientist, was a country landowner who chose to spend his life at Fyne Court, the ancestral seat in Somerset; and there he died, in the room in which both he and his father had been born. Llewelyn

Powys said of his roving years: 'It was always to the fells around Dunkery Beacon that my dreams would go . . .' Elgar said that people who believed in ghosts might one day look for him on the Malverns of his native Worcestershire. A King of England, George V, said of his Norfolk home: 'Dear old Sandringham, the place I love best in all the world.' Such roots are old as well as deep. Ruth wept because she felt homesick; and when the poet Horace received the gift of a small farm he returned thanks in verse: 'This was one of my dreams . . . a little bit of land with a garden; near the house, a spring of living water; and beside it a small wood. Heaven has fulfilled that dream, more generously than I had ever hoped.'

From time immemorial a norm, though those avowals may soon sound like aberrations. Nevertheless, the avowals were made, and some of the makers survived into the second half of the twentieth century. John Masefield, born and bred at Ledbury, affirmed: 'The Herefordshire scene had its part in making me, and was a profound influence on my work.' Flora Thompson admitted that the threads which bound her to Oxfordshire were 'spun of love and kinship and cherished memories'. A Welsh poet, R. S. Thomas, countered the fashionable fallacy that ephemeral roots are better than perdurable ones: 'It is in learning to love and cherish our own little tree or brook that we become fitted for wider and deeper affections.' To emphasize the point once again, long residence in the same parish is bound to become exceptional at a time when many people are uprooted by economic necessity. While increasing the number of nomads, technology has decreased the number of farmfolk, thereby challenging G. M. Trevelyan's belief that 'Agriculture is not merely one industry among many, but a way of life, unique and *irreplaceable* in its human and splendid virtues.' Another voice in the wilderness was H. J. Massingham's, who cited the physical and psychological nourishment that is supplied by roots delving deep into 'Those lanes which lead to what the world calls nowhere, namely, the hamlets, villages, and farms, the cornerstones of England.'

A Quiet Season

People who are able to escape the rigours of a British winter must use several words with which to announce their departure for Madeira or South Africa. In that respect the Romans were more economic. When the frost-bitten Governor of a British province retreated awhile to Egypt or Provence, he described his sun-seeking succinctly with a single word, *Hiberno*, meaning 'I am going to winter quarters'. If, however, we refer to warmth-seeking animals, we become as succinct as the Romans, saying simply 'hibernation' or a profound sleep which reduces bodily movement and therefore the need to find food wherewith to sustain life. Very few British fauna hibernate throughout the winter. Bats do, and dormice; but squirrels and tortoises wake up now and again (if they remain awake too long, cold weather will kill them). Animal metabolism can vary dramatically with circumstances. When a chipmunk is active it takes one hundred breaths every minute, yet during hibernation it takes only one breath every five minutes.

Gilbert White's Sussex tortoise began retreating in late autumn. 'It retires underground', he reported, 'about the middle of November, and comes forth again about the middle of April.' White watched the tortoise's laborious bed-making: 'It scrapes out the ground with its forefeet and throws it up over its back with the hind . . .' On one occasion the weather became so warm that the bed-making tortoise 'was continually interrupted, and called forth by the heat in the middle of the day. . .'. Having at last scooped and settled into what White called a 'hybernaculum', the tortoise was not amused when White roused it: 'I dug it out of its winter dormitory last March, when it was enough awakened to express resentment by hissing . . .' After an eighty-mile journey to Selborne (travelling in a box which White himself designed), the tortoise was jolted into wakefulness: 'It walked twice down to the bottom of my garden; however, in the evening, the weather being cold, it buried itself in the loose mould, and continued still concealed.' That was on 21 April 1780.

Not long afterwards, White noticed the effect of the rising

temperature: 'The tortoise heaved up the mould and put out its head; and next morning came forth, as if it were raised from the dead; and walked about till four in the afternoon.' White was not among those scientists who flinch whenever anybody suggests that life pursues a purpose. He was a theodicist or believer that life does pursue a purpose albeit one whose ultimate result we cannot even imagine. Despite his faith as an Anglican priest, White did regard the long-living tortoise with an astonishment which came close to a rebuke: 'It is a matter of wonder to find that Providence should bestow such a profusion of days, such a seeming waste of longevity, on a reptile that appears to relish it so little as to squander two thirds of its existence in a joyless stupor, and to be lost to all sensation for months together in the profoundest slumbers.'

Although I would never accuse them of lapsing into a joyless stupor, I do feel that the inhabitants of certain holiday resorts tend—as the Irishman put it—to hibernate in summer. When I last visited such a place, during August, the steep lane was flanked by fields full of caravans, some of whose transistors were blaring rival cacophonies. Since parking within the village is almost impossible in summer, I left my car on the edge of the parish. The narrow streets, I found, were crammed with visitors staring into gift shops, sports shops, tea shops, antique shops. The small seaside promenade was a queue of semi-stationary vehicles, frequently impeded by motorists waiting for other motorists to quit their parking place. Speed-boats in the harbour made it difficult to converse without shouting. Then a motor coach arrived—I shuddered to imagine its progress down the steep lane—whereupon all traffic halted while people emerged from their cars and began shouting at one another. Although it was past noon, several youths and girls were sleeping in a quayside shelter.

Waiting to cross the street, I heard a woman say to her companion: 'Last year we went to Spain, but as my husband is still on strike we thought it would be wiser just to have a fortnight in this place. It's all right for a weekend, but I'd go crazy living here all the year round. What on earth do they do during the winter?' I felt tempted to reply: 'During the winter they wake up. They stroll quietly along the promenade, and they park their car without difficulty. Instead of queueing at the shops, they arrive when they please and spend some time chatting with the shopkeeper. Instead of being disturbed by slammed doors and shrill gearboxes at midnight, they sleep to the sound of the waves.'

Outside the bakery I met a friend who said: 'Normally I never go out at this hour. In fact, we usually try to get away during August. Believe it or not, I've just come from the bread queue.'

Walking uphill to the car, I heard a visitor say: 'Between September and Easter the place must be dead.' Again I felt tempted to reply: 'On the contrary, it is then that the place comes alive. The villagers attend their literary soirée, their music club, their archaeological film show, lifeboat fund dance, handicraft session, lace-making class, gardening quiz, Baptist coffee morning, Catholic mothers' afternoon, parish choir practice, old folks' whist drive, under-fives' fun hour, amateur dramatic society, west country gleemen, yoga-for-all, arthritics' chair race, naval old comrades' night. In fact', I almost said, 'It's a wonder they have time to sleep at all.'

Browsing in the Rain

Finding myself in a small country town, with an hour to wait until the branch line train arrived, I proposed to spend the time exploring the church, the guildhall, and any other features of the town I had never before visited. On this occasion, however, a violent storm led me to shelter in a second-hand bookshop, where the titles of some of the books sounded so strange that I jotted them down: *Confessions of an Enquiring Spirit*, *Perils Afloat* and *Brigands Ashore*, *The Art of Cooking by Gas.*

Several of the books came from Cassell's sixpenny library, first published in 1889, and their gilt lettering was as bright as that on some of the books that were published in 1982. The advertisements in the series would nowadays cause an incredulous shake of the head. Robinson and Cleaver, for example, offered Irish linen table napkins at three old pence apiece, with shirts at £1.50 per half dozen. A box of Wright's coal tar soap cost five new pence.

Scarcely able to believe my eyes, I noticed a first edition of the Hon. John Fortescue's *Records of Stag-Hunting on Exmoor*, splendidly illustrated, embossed with vivid gold title, and weighing at least two pounds. The price was 10p. Had the owner of the shop been present he would surely have detected the mistaken price. As it was, a young girl accepted the coin, saying simply: 'It seems to have stopped raining.' It had indeed, and I felt tempted to explore the town, but since the railway station stood some distance away, I decided to remain where I was, not trusting the piebald sky. In any event, a customer who had already made a purchase could not fairly be accused of outstaying his welcome. Thus it was that I found a book whose vast size suggested that it ranked among Lamb's books that are not books, 'biblia a-biblia—Court Calendars, Directories,

Scientific Treatises, Almanacks, Statutes at Large . . .'. The book proved to be a loosely bound paste-up of newspaper cuttings which someone had collected. The price was £5, which seemed as absurd as the 10p for Fortescue's rare and handsome volume.

The shop girl having retired to an inner office, I felt at liberty to copy some of the cuttings, beginning with a Kentish newspaper which in 1804 reported a visit by the Prime Minister: 'On Thursday last Mr Pitt, accompanied by Generals Twiss and Moore, met the Lords and bailiff of the level of Romney Marsh at New Hall near Dymchurch, to consider the best mode of inundating the Marsh in case of invasion.' Another cutting, from a Kentish newspaper in 1940, contained the following item: 'The vicar ended his address by reminding Hitler that Romney Marsh had defied an earlier dictator, Napoleon.' In 1805 a west country newspaper stated: 'Yesterday morning the Packet boat hove-to, half a mile off shore, to signal a great victory by Admiral Nelson at Cape Trafalgar.' The packet had received the signal from a frigate which in turn had received it from the *Victory* at a time when, although success was assured, news of Nelson's mortal wound remained a secret; so, the readers' jubilation was soon eclipsed by a nation's sorrow.

Somewhat to my surprise the shop girl appeared with two cups of tea, one of which she offered to me. 'Well,' I said, 'it's very kind of you, but I've only spent 10p.'

'That doesn't matter,' she replied, 'the boss never expects to make money. He bought the shop for his wife, really. They set the loss against their profits from the catering trade.'

Before leaving, I had time to examine several faded collections of essays about the English countryside a century ago. They were of two sorts, those that dealt chiefly with flora and fauna, and those that ranged more widely. Both sorts began to appear when the industrialized Victorians created a demand for them; and the second sort depicted characters whose heirs and successors have not yet become unrecognizable as shepherds, gamekeepers, blacksmiths, eccentric spinsters, hard-riding squires, feckless younger sons, country parsons, rich businessmen, retired colonels, village schoolmasters, envious levellers. Many of the essays were examples of what Walter de la Mare called 'writing that is pitched above the voice'. Others seemed first-rate, among them being a technical piece about pig keeping, written by Richard Jefferies for a magazine; and also an idyllic evocation of an early morning voyage on an Oxfordshire river, written by Edward Thomas when he was an exhibitioner at Lincoln College.

Whether the girl then offered me a biscuit as an inducement to buy those books I cannot say; but I did invest a small sum in a copy of Sir Arthur Quiller-Couch's *Poems and Ballads*, for which, half an hour later, a passenger in the train made an unsuccessful bid of £5. The book itself was published in 1896 and is now worth a sizeable amount to Q's admirers. Only last week, in fact, a Barnstaple literary man was offering £10 for a copy in reasonable condition, but my own copy still remains mine. My other investment was in a collection of the country essays which Sir William Beach Thomas used to write for a Sunday newspaper. Glancing at the sodden landscape, I felt that one quotation from the book was very seasonable. 'The sighs for sunshine in our literature are as a hundred to one of the sighs for rain.'

A Distant Prospect

For years and years I used to look at it and wonder how on earth anyone could reach it. My first sighting was made from the lane to Hutton Roof, with the little town of Kirkby Lonsdale cupped invisible far below; and beyond it Barbon High Fell, surging like the ramparts of a fabled city; and on the right of those ramparts—miles away, in another county—there it stood, a small farmhouse near the summit of a Westmorland fell.

Few other English dwellings are set in such bleak and lofty solitude. Often I had seen the squat stone house beside a few acres of hayfield. On winter evenings I could just discern one lamplit window, a mere speck, smaller than a glow-worm, shining bravely in a world of darkness. On summer mornings the hayfield resembled a bowling green in a desert of rock and swamp. The closest I came to it was when I climbed the No Through Road to Bullpot Farm, which had been a track until a nobleman built a shooting lodge under the brow of Barbon Low Fell, whence the wilderness slopes steeply before soaring to the farmhouse on the far side of the ravine; but the house itself was so distant that, although I sometimes saw, I could never hear, a tractor working there.

Did I really wonder how on earth anyone could reach such a place? Part of me probably did wonder, but another part must have known very well how to reach the place, for I had explored all the lanes a dozen miles around and had walked many of the paths and tracks. Nevertheless, during those decades of distant sightings I neither visited the place nor troubled to find the way thither. Not long ago, while climbing to Bullpot, I halted, as was my custom, and looked across at the farm, and for the umpteenth time I saw the vivid hayfield and one window winking at the sun. It was then that I resolved to visit the place. Next morning, therefore, I drove across the Lancashire border to Cowan Bridge, where a row of cottages used to be the Clergy Daughters' School, a well-intentioned but meanly-administered charity, founded by a local clergyman, Carus Wilson, and attended by Charlotte Brönte, who depicted it as Lowood, a place of penance rather than a cradle of content. Nowadays the school is at Casterton, well administered and well esteemed.

From Cowan Bridge a lane reached the parish of Leck (Saxon *lece* meaning stream). There is a stately house at Leck, seat of the Shuttleworth family, but beyond it there are very few houses indeed, and after a mile or so there are no houses at all. Twisting and climbing, the lane became narrower, bumpier, lonelier. Fortunately, I was accompanied by an elderly Westmorlander who warned me not to proceed too far lest I shared the fate of a holidaymaker who did proceed too far, smashed his headlights and wings while trying to turn back, got bogged down, walked through rain to a distant telephone, and eventually paid £310 for the towing and repair of his vehicle. On, then, we went, higher and higher, until I began to wonder not how, but why, anyone ever reached the place. Left and right the land grew steeper and drearier. Trees were fewer and more stunted. The herbage was coarse and embrowned. Down in the valley the October sunshine had warmed us, but on the fells a wind whined.

'It's the deuce of a way from the nearest shop,' my companion said. 'Yet I can remember when the family had no car, no telephone, no radio, and a track that would make this one seem like a main road. Ingleton they went to.' He glanced over his shoulder, as though he could see through the hillside. 'Ingleton,' he repeated. 'In those years it was a busy little market town, but nowadays people drive to Kendal or Settle . . . even to Manchester, some of 'em.'

Presently I stopped, and got out, and thought how strange it was, to stand within a mile of the place which I had often seen from a distance, and for the first time to look across at Barbon Low Fell which I had often climbed. Below, the River Lune looped blue loops *en route* for Morecambe and the sea, visible far astern. On the opposite side of the ravine I saw Bullpot Farm and one other small farmhouse, neither of which is permanently occupied. Years ago, I thought, the trio must have kept one another company, if only via their lamplit windows.

Continuing on foot, we paused now and again to stare at the ravine on our left, where Lost John's Cave served as a warning to potholers. Not wishing to appear inquisitive, I stopped short of the house, but was able to see it near and clear, a dour little eyrie, though to its occupants a kindly one despite the inclement solitude. Scanning the desolate landscape, my companion said: 'I've seen wagons and horses up here, carting coal from a shallow working. Must be seventy years ago now. My grandfather told me that the family were snowbound for weeks on end. More than one man's been found dead in a drift up here.'

'It's chilly,' I replied. 'Let's turn back.'

With a sense of having belatedly achieved something, we walked down to the car and were glad to see trees again, flamboyant in autumnal sunlight. Small though it was, Leck village seemed to be the hub of a populous universe. When next I climb to Bullpot and gaze at the distant farm I shall feel that I am not wholly a stranger to Leck Fell House.

11

A Memorable Cup of Tea

While walking in wintry twilight I was reminded of two short walks that were made in similar conditions. Each of them led me to a memorable cup of tea. The first walk, during World War II, was in response to an invitation from an eminent poet living in Buckinghamshire. The house, his letter said, stood at the end of an avenue. Petrol being rationed, I cycled the fifteen miles from my own home, past furrowed fields, and smoke climbing above cottage chimneys. I dismounted some way short of the house, and proceeded on foot. Although in those years every house was blacked out after dark, I could not help feeling that his house wore an empty look. Three times I knocked, and three times the echo went unanswered. The silence recalled the traveller in a famous poem: 'Is there anybody there?' Wondering whether I had mistaken the time and place, I reread the invitation. No; I was at the right place at the right time. I had already turned back when I heard, or though I heard, a sound from the house. This time I walked past the door, hoping to find another entrance; and again I heard, or thought I heard, a sound. Glancing over my shoulder, I saw Walter de la Mare advancing through the dusk 'Forgive my old ears,' he said. A few moments later we entered a small room, and after some preliminary conversation my host went away and presently returned with the tea tray.

Everything seemed in keeping with the man . . . fey, dreamlike, yet keenly aware of his surroundings. It was indeed a remarkable experience, sitting with an elderly poet, alone in a large house encircled by silence and trees. When he asked about my war service, I replied that I was now performing inconspicuous duties ashore. 'Nevertheless,' he said, almost enviously, 'they *are* duties.' Some years later he wrote a poem, called 'England', which explained his remark to me:

> Through two dark crises in thy Fate I have lived—
> But—never fought for thee.

Walter de la Mare moved and spoke with Victorian dignity, and had known many of the writers of his time. We both admired Mary Webb, of whom he wrote some words that were true of himself also: 'She loved to listen to other people talking as much as to talk, but her own talk had an extraordinary eagerness and vivacity.'

Of my journey home, under a frosty sky, I remember only that, even at the time, I remembered nothing. My thoughts were all of a frail seer, alone among dusky woods, in a land which he served with his pen:

> No lovelier hills than thine have laid
> My tired thoughts to rest:
> No peace of lovelier valleys made
> Like peace within my breast.

The second walk, a few years later, was in response to an invitation from the Poet Laureate, John Masefield, whose Oxfordshire estate sloped to the Thames at Clifton Hampden, near the Barley Mow, an inn made famous by those three men in a boat: the quaintest, most otherworldly inn up the river . . . its low-pitched gables and thatched roof and lattice windows gave it a story-book appearance . . .'.

Setting out from the Chilterns, I soon sighted the Berkshire hills, growing dimmer as the light failed. Very little traffic appeared on the lanes, and lamplight already shone from wayside cottages and farms. When I halted, to exercise the dog, I heard a woman calling the cows home. Again my destination stood at the end of a tree-lined drive, so I left the car beside the lodge gates and continued on foot, feeling diffident at the prospect of meeting an eminent poet, an honorary Master Mariner, and a former Midshipman RNR.

Near the front door I noticed a middle-aged woman about to enter the house. Since she seemed surprised to see me, I said: 'Dr Masefield is expecting me.' Then it was my own turn to feel surprised, because, instead of inviting me to enter, the woman opened the front door and called: 'Father, a man's called to mend the gas.' The mistake having been rectified, Masefield himself appeared—tall, courteous, benign—explaining that he really was expecting someone to mend the gas. 'Fortunately,' he smiled, 'we are still able to boil a kettle.'

At that meeting, the first of many, I asked Masefield whether he had ever met Thomas Hardy, a naïve question even from a man who was still relatively young. Masefield replied by turning to his wife: 'When did we last see Tom?' I remember also a sense of awe when he referred to W. B. Yeats as 'Willie'. Above all, I remember his gesture when he stood on the doorstep, with one arm raised to bid an unimportant guest *au revoir*. This he continued to do until our final meeting, a quarter of a century later, when he was too weak to move.

The journey home passed quickly. The fields, I remember, glistened with frost, and on the summit of the Chilterns, somewhere near Looseley Row, an isolated window shone as though it were a lighthouse. Even before meeting him, I knew that Masefield's career had not been a carefree rise to fame. Wide recognition eluded him for many years, and his only son died young. Nevertheless, the impression that I formed on that wintry evening remains unchanged, for Masefield kept his faith in life, expressing it with a single line:

> Somewhere in every heart it's April still.

Roman Candles

Although they tend to keep to themselves they still retain something of their former role as leaders in local society. If a label were required, it might classify them as members of the ancient Catholic gentry. The family's Angevin ancestors held fifteen manors and a fortified house, but the estate has dwindled to less than four hundred acres, and the present people are sometimes compelled to sell a Stubbs or perhaps a piece of Fabergé which their forebears received from the Czar. When the last trinket went, the lady of the house said: 'Well, it'll help to pay Stonyhurst for the next few years.'

The family's allegiance to the Sovereign was proven at the time of the Armada, when a younger son served under the Lord High Admiral, Howard of Effingham. Unfortunately, another son plotted to assassinate Queen Elizabeth I and to re-impose a religion which the majority of his compatriots detested as alien, tyrannical, and superstitious. Fighting literally for her life, the Queen had no choice but to make an example of the traitor. He was executed, and most of the estates were sold to pay a huge fine. Like all their co-religionists in England, the family were forbidden to vote, to hold a commission in the Armed Forces, to attend either of the two great universities, or to play any significant part in the life of their country. When at last Sir Robert Peel introduced a Catholic Emancipation Bill the family repaired the severed links with Oxford. They then begat a brace of naval officers and after that they unseated a Liberal at a general election, but they never regained their pre-Reformation status. However, they preserved the domestic chapel, and some of the neighbouring Roman Catholics attend Mass there. Tradition says that G. K. Chesterton tried to attend, but found that the fourteenth-century doorway was slimmer than his waistline.

After their disastrous lapse into treason the family trod warily, though without ever becoming Trimmers, not even to the winds from the Curia. During the 1870s, for example, they shared Lord Acton's opposition to the doctrine of papal infallibility. In short—unlike many of the intellectual converts—they never became *plus papiste que le Pape*. At the same time they remain conservative. Like their Tudor forebears, they insist that every ordained member of the English Church is a layman, unhallowed by the apostolic succession. They shun all priests who speak lightly of celibacy and also of bishops whose authority cannot be confounded by a show of hands. They prefer the Latin to the anglicized liturgy, and although they join with Jews and Baptists on Remembrance Sunday, they do not allow a non-Romanist to take part in the conduct of their own services. A kinsman, an aged Monsignor, formerly employed in Rome, now lives with the family and acts as chaplain, librarian, and archivist. He has already published a selection of the family correspondence, which was well received as 'a valuable contribution to our knowledge of the role of the rural gentry during the early sixteenth century.' Forty years ago, while staying as a guest, the same kinsman earned the family's gratitude by discovering and identifying a Dutch landscape in a loft above the servants' bedrooms. At a London auction the painting fetched enough money to re-roof the house and to instal electricity and main drainage. Less profitable, though to some historians more interesting, was the discovery of a priests' hide-out which the family had built during the last year of Henry VIII's reign. Concealed under a paving stone in the kitchen, the place went unnoticed until the new drains were dug. Despite lack of reliable evidence, there is a tradition that Edmund Campion hid there for six days and nights while the Sheriff's men searched in vain.

Despite the secular age in which they live, the family continue to encounter what is at best suspicion and at worst hostility. The suspicion comes chiefly from people who are reasonably tolerant and adequately educated; the hostility comes chiefly from the ignorant masses and the rabid Protestants. The masses believe that every Roman Catholic worships the Virgin Mary; that every Roman Catholic regards incense as a necessary milestone on the road to Heaven; and that every Roman Catholic will support any insurrection which enjoys a papal *nil obstat*. The family can accept the suspicion, but the hostility distresses them because they know that it is ancient and was well founded. At school and at Oxford they learn of Langland's anger against mediaeval papal interference in English affairs. They learn of the scandals within the Papacy itself, exemplified by the rivalry between Rome and Avignon. They learn of the papal blessing which sailed with an Armada that was to conquer England, to murder or to depose the Queen, and to deploy the dreaded Inquisition against any who would not abjure the English Church. They learn also of their co-religionists—laity and priesthood alike—who in foreign parts conspired and still do conspire to be no friends of England. Against that suspicion the family set their own loyal Englishry, confident that neither Rome nor Whitehall is likely ever to divide it. Seeing all around them a greedy and godless egalitarianism, they murmur 'Amen' to the prediction of Hilaire Belloc who said: 'Our civilization is splitting more and more into two camps, and what was common to the whole of it is becoming restricted to the Christian, and will soon be restricted to the Catholic half.'

Not everyone agrees with such special pleading. The villagers' attitude was expressed by the Anglican rector, himself a High Churchman, who, on the eve of the Pope's visit to Britain preached a sermon against bigotry and all other uncharitableness, and ended by quoting part of the thirty-seventh Article in the Book of Common Prayer: 'The Bishop of Rome hath no jurisdiction in this Realm of England.'

The Dark Days

In heavy rain I watched him trimming the hedges of his smallholding. Wielding a billhook, he made a neat job of it, unlike the machines which always bruise the branches, often miss the brambles, and usually leave the litter. After a midday meal, he returned to collect and burn the debris. At four o'clock, when the light was fading, he walked half a mile to fetch his three cows, and then half a mile home. Having milked the cows, he walked a mile downhill to join the bell-ringers. During that same week he spent not less than thirty hours in the open air, heedless of wind and rain.

It is true that much farm-work is now done by machines, some of which are fitted with weatherproof cabs. It is true that many farm-hands drive to and from the fields in warm cars. It is also true that in the pre-mechanical days an incalculable

amount of time and energy was wasted on walking and heaving and pitching. Nevertheless, farm life is still open air life, and those who follow it are exposed to the elements in ways which people in offices and factories would reject as intolerable. Members of the farming community do not as a rule work in a centrally heated building, nor do they seize every opportunity to avoid extremes of temperature. They are more likely to sweat while mowing a meadow, to shiver while thawing a trough, to spend hours on a mountain or—if they live near the sea—at the helm of a fishing boat; and they do those things not once or twice for fun, but many times a year because their livelihood demands it. They never regard the weather as a mere topic of conversation, relevant only to fuel bills and holidays. Physically, emotionally, and financially, the weather is an important part of their life.

'When everything else has failed', wrote Beethoven, 'there is always the countryside.' He meant, of course, that only the most grievous calamity will destroy a countryman's ability to draw consolation from the sights and sounds of rural life. For Beethoven the consolation was not merely aesthetic; it was—like Noah's dove—a promise that all manner of things would ultimately be well. In lighter mood, when at a loss for small-talk, countryfolk may re-phrase Beethoven's adage as: 'When everything else has failed, there is always the weather.' The topic itself, however, need not become a source of platitudinous trivia; on the contrary, it may devise a quiz: 'I have just put some more logs on the fire. The rain sounds nearly as loud as the wind. What is the date?' The answer may be either: 'Christmas Eve' or 'Midsummer Day'. The quiz can continue as follows: 'I am sipping coffee in the garden while admiring the roses. What is the month and where is the garden?' Valid answers may then be either 'July in Aberdeenshire' or 'January in Devonshire'. Whether in north-east Scotland or in south-west England, November is a dark season. The flowerbeds are barren, the meadows are muddy, the woodlands are leafless; and although botanists may detect signs of rebirth, the ordinary countryman looks in vain for any sign of spring.

When the winning post is at last in sight, a weary athlete may unleash the spurt that gives him victory, but November offers no such incentive to people who already feel the onset of winter's darkness and perhaps the remembrance of a disappointing summer. The novelty of buttered toast by firelight has worn off; so, too, has the novelty of breakfasting by lamplight, of exercising the dog by starlight, and of stumbling to the woodshed without any light at all. Despite the land's lean look, however, the seasons do overlap, each being a tomb that contains its sire, and a womb that gestates its heir.

When the sun shines furrows gleam like molten chocolate, and shadows cover half the length of a long field. Midges loop the loop in a shaft of amber light. Trees justify the poet:

> How fair and bare and lovely-clear
> The burnished branches bend and veer
> Toward the ending of the year.
> How chipped and shorn the byeways stand,
> New-levelled by a hedger's hand.

Impatient with the year's slow decease, you may feel tempted to stir the soil in search of a daffodil, or to listen for a thrush. The temptation, however, must be resisted. To seek the spring in November is as premature as to cast a clout in May. Unlike Job's latter end, the year's penultimate month is not often sunny or serene; and even when the winter has passed, and the time of the singing of birds has come, still we may suffer the winds in March, the snow in April, the frost in May, the sleet in June, the drought in July, the deluge in August. When Coleridge hoped that all seasons would eventually seem dear to his infant son, he did not require the child to greet every season with equal affection. On the contrary, he himself wrote a poem cursing the muddy Devon roads:

> The indignant Bard composed this furious ode,
> As tired he dragged his way thro' Plimtree road!

In a week or two we shall be able to console ourselves by knowing that the days will soon begin to lengthen; but at present they are still dwindling, and with them our patience.

Zoological Gardens

I am not surprised to learn that several private zoos have lately gone into liquidation. My own zoo sometimes threatens to eat itself into indigence. I say 'my own zoo' because certain of the inmates really do belong to me. Some of the others—birds, stags, shrews, badgers—belong to themselves; and a few are owned by a neighbouring farm. My zoo includes a dog, a cat, the farmer's shire horse, and a flock of his sheep which graze my small fields and thereby keep the grass in fair condition. To begin with, only the sheep were admitted, but by that time the grass was almost too tall for their taste, so that patches of potential hay appeared. Instead of scything, therefore, I invited the shire horse, and within a week he had lowered the level to suit the sheep. After another week the level became too low, so the horse went into the smaller field, which has a wire fence but is not large enough to justify the cost of sheep netting. In that field the herbage between April and October will support the horse for about a week.

Sheep may be silly, but they are no fools. On first arriving here they regarded the Jack Russell as a kind of itinerant abattoir. The mere sight of him caused them to huddle in a far corner, bumping against a drystone wall that can withstand the weather but not the wethers. After a day or two the sheep perceived that the dog had been taught not to worry them. At the moment, as I glance through the window, the dog sits beside the netting while the sheep graze placidly. Cats they seem not to notice. Tinker, a black-and-white one, adopts all manner of tigrine postures, but the sheep ignore him. In saying that sheep are silly, we mean—or ought to mean—that they are gregarious and (except in defence of their young) timid. I witnessed an example of the herd instinct earlier this morning, when one of the ewes failed to notice that the others had moved from my own field into a larger one belonging to the farmer. When the ewe looked up and saw that she was alone, she uttered a shrill bleat and ran full-speed in search of her sisters. Like children, sheep seem rather to acquire than to inherit some of their timidity, for whereas an old ram may give you a nasty look and then back away, a young lamb will stare, evidently puzzled—but not yet terrified—by the strange inhabitants of its brave new world. If you move quietly and slowly, the creature will let you come close. If you keep it as a pet, it will soon become an adhesive nuisance.

A second glance through the window shows the zoo assembled in the upper field, together with the farmer's dogs. A rook is there, a jay, a heron, a pheasant, two pigeons, several smaller birds, and a squirrel. These, of course, are not the only occupants of my zoological garden. Goldfish explore the pool, worms aerate the soil, and an army of insects go about their business invisibly, inaudibly, innumerably. The scene, in fact, recalls the Norfolk property of Captain Marryat, author of *Mr Midshipman Easy* and several other novels. When Theodore Hook visited Marryat he found 'animals everywhere; calves were feeding on the lawn; ponies and a donkey under a clump of larches; a colt and its mama. There were coops of fowls standing in the gravel path . . .'. Marryat's children shared his love of fauna. According to Hook, a jackdaw 'sat on the shoulder of one of the little girls, and as the party neared the lawn, it was joined by a number of pigeons . . . there were also an aviary, rabbits, pheasants, partridges, cats, dogs, and donkeys . . . In the walled garden a tame seagull . . .' The smallest of the girls was fondling a rat which had lately killed a ferret. One wonders whether Hook approved this mingling of the species; he was undoubtedly taken aback by it. At least the birds and animals were not caged, as in a modern zoo, where some people like to see lions and elephants pacing up and down the few yards of a cell.

Since the word 'zoo' comes from the Greek *zoos*, meaning 'life', it follows that every garden is zoological. My own teems with ants, bees, butterflies, hedgehogs, moths, slugs, snails, spiders, wasps, and sundry other species, some of which are known only to the people who study them. Many human beings prefer to forget that most creatures eat one another in order to live, which seems a gruesome arrangement, but was none of our doing and cannot be changed by us. Even if we deliberately refrain from eating other creatures, we are often compelled to kill them in defence of our fruits, flowers, crops, and vegetables. When dealing with animals, some people find it difficult to steer a middle way between folly and cruelty. At Nether Stowey, for example, Coleridge occupied a house infested with mice. 'They play the very Devil with us,' he complained; yet he could not bring himself to set traps, because the mice were his guests, and to kill them would be, as he put it, 'a foul breach of hospitality'. For the same reason he refused to kill certain plants, saying: 'The weeds have taken liberty to grow, and I thought it unfair in me to prejudice the soil towards roses and strawberries.' Like a strict Jain, Coleridge would have gone bankrupt had he taken to market gardening.

My own worst enemy is a mole. It arrived shortly after one of the lawns had been levelled and returfed. Within a few days the surface resembled a sponge, covered with erupting boils. Traps were set, and the mole bypassed them. More traps were set, and this time the mole dug them up. I once kept watch for three hours, hoping to sight and slay the sinner, but nothing appeared until I went indoors to answer the telephone. On returning, I found a new mound and a circle of stones. Since Progress has eliminated the village vermin-catcher, and since strychnine cannot be obtained over the counter, the pest continues to mock the sympathizers who have kindly recommended their own bizarre methods of mole catching.

All in a Day's Work

We were trimming a hedge. More precisely, James trimmed while I collected the debris. It was a bright morning, late autumn at its best, with an ornamental sun beaming from skies swept clear by a brisk nor'wester. Everything that could shine, did so; and ivy on the trees glistened like wet seaweed. If you kept moving you kept warm. If you stood still you felt cold and began to shiver. We worked at the edge of my lower paddock, overlooking a combe that is wide and yet so deep that the

stream in the depths of it could be heard but not seen. Very faint it sounded, like wavelets on a distant shore. Nothing stirred except the wind booming through bare boughs. Although James is nearly eighty years old, he stood on top of the embankment, slashing left and right in a manner which townsfolk would regard as recklessly careless. Actually, his arm and eyes were all the while co-ordinating the attack, confident as Robert Bridges's athlete whose

> every perfect action hath the grace
> Of indolence or thoughtless hardihood . . .

With a precision which seemed uncanny, James checked each downward stroke so that a branch was only partly lopped. Likewise, with the blade already falling, he detected the timber that must be severed. I had learned the same craft long ago, but my farm tutelage lasted scarcely three months, and I still need to grasp any branches which require only a slight incision. James, by contrast, relied solely on wrist and eye, working gloveless and without spectacles, his rosy cheeks reddened by the wind. He seldom spoke while working, and never paused in order to chatter. Having planned the next phase of a task, he fulfilled it; only then would he take a brief rest. During one such interlude he straightened his back, saying: 'I once saw a ewe with eight legs.'

'Eight?' I exclaimed, uncertain whether he were joking.

'Eight,' he repeated. 'I took a picture of 'en. 'Twas a proper sight. More like a centipede than a sheep.'

'Did the ewe survive?'

'Her did an' all. They had the vet to 'en. Amputated the unnecessary supernumeraries, as you might say. 'Tisn't every farmer would have bothered. But old Tom Molton he fair loved his sheep. He once said to me, "James", he said, "I'd ha' done the same for a glow-worm". I knew Tom near sixty years, and never once did I see 'en strike a dumb creature, though I own he kept his three sons to heel. Not that he was soft, mind. I've heard 'en cuss a collie in language that would ha' made the Bible sound downright prudish. "O thou something-something!" he shouted. "O thou brainless product of an un'oly mating! O thou unregenerate offspring of an unprintable bitch!" Had the prophets by heart, did old Tom Molton. Maybe that's why the vicar chosen 'en for his warden.'

James paused to whet the blade. 'I always remember . . . mind out, that branch is going to swing back . . . remember the day when Tom went to collect a joint o' meat for the vicarage. Davey were the butcher in them years. Not a particular man, Davey, 'cept when it came to sending the bill. Any'ow, Tom didn't like the look o' that joint, nor the smell neither, so the two men had a few words, and the finish was, Tom said, "Curate's egg be damned. This yere's the vicar's fatted calf. And what's he going to say when he sees 'en? I'll tell 'ee. He's going to say, I wouldn't even offer it to Sodom and all the other cities o' the plain".'

'So what happened?'

''Twas simple. Tom chucked the meat on the floor and then he bid his dog take a bite, and do you know, her wouldn't touch the stuff. Just backed away, Tom said. I own it sounds a tall story, but in 1920 the butcher didn't have no fridge, and anyway Tom wouldn't ha' lied. I've heard 'en say, "When you'm telling a story don't 'ee go titivating same, 'cause you've only to look around in real life and you'll find more miracles than was ever recorded in the Book of Akopalypse."'

'I rather think the Book is called . . .'

''Tis called Apocalypse. But that's a word poor Tom never could get his tongue to. That and the men in the fiery furnace. Shakhad, Micah, and Abednegro . . . Tom called 'em something different every time. In the end he gave up and just said, "They three fellas with the fancy names". There'll be a frost tonight.' James addressed the last remark to the sky, which was becoming clearer and less windy.

When he had gone home to supper, I piled the barrow with the last load of briars, bracken, twigs, branches, weeds, and a gumboot that must have lain there above a dozen years. Except for the wind, it was quieter than ever now and growing colder. Using a dung-fork, I stacked the trimmings in two adjacent heaps, choosing a site that would not send smoke across the house. Then I went back to inspect James's handiwork, admiring yet again the craftsmanship he had learned sixty years ago and still practised with unassuming pride. After that, I returned to light the bonfires. Paper, dry kindling, a sprinkle of paraffin, a match, a whoof! And then a crackle as the flames leapt up, emitting sparks that soared like airborne rubies through the dusk. Presently the wind dropped, but the two fires still warmed my face.

Prometheus, they say, gave fire to mankind. Certainly the cavemen must have welcomed his gift while they crouched half-naked through a frosty night, hearing the hungry wolves, watching the falling snow. Something of their awe welled up in me as the incandescent pyre subsided into a mound of ashes, fringed by the tips of smouldering twigs.

12

Food for Thought

When the trained stopped at Banbury I noticed that boys no longer walked up and down the platform, selling Banbury cakes. Sixty years ago I watched and helped to increase, their brisk trade. Richard Braithwaite remarked that Banbury was famous for 'Ale, Zeal, Cakes and Cheese'. Shakespeare, if I remember, mentioned the cheese, and Jonson mentioned the zeal alias Zeal-in-the-Land-Busy, a fanatical Banbury baker and Lord's Day observer:

> To Banbury came I, O profane one,
> Where I met a Puritane one
> Hanging of his cat on Monday
> For killing of a mouse on Sunday.

At this season, when shops overflow with succulent titbits, one could compile a long list of dishes bearing a topographical name; Bakewell tart, Yorkshire pudding, Lancashire hotpot, Cornish pasty, Devonshire split, Dorset cob, Dover sole, Welsh rarebit, Aylesbury duckling, Norfolk dumpling, Cumbrian sausage, Stilton cheese, Bath bun. Concerning Bath buns the most I can discover amounts to very little indeed, namely, that at an unspecified date an anonymous Bath baker produced and made popular a bun studded with sugar crystals. Bath Oliver biscuits, on the other hand, possess a veritable pedigree showing that they were invented by an eighteenth-century Bath physician, Dr William Oliver, FRS, for the benefit of patients who took much Bath water but hardly any Bath food.

Unlike Bath buns, Stilton cheese confronts the genealogist with a plethora of pedigrees. Stilton itself used to be a staging post on the Great North Road, but a bypass now allows the villagers to live at some distance from the din of lorries and cars. Again unlike Bath buns, Stilton cheese did *not* originate at its place-name. When Celia Fiennes visited Stilton in 1696 her journal made no mention of the cheese. John Nichols, the eighteenth-century historian, claimed that it was invented in 1730 by a Mrs Orton of Little Dalby in Leicestershire. 'At first', he explained, 'it was supposed that it could be made only from the milk of cows fed in one close, now called Orton Close, but this was afterwards found to be an error.' Against that, if you visit the Leicestershire hamlet of Withcote (an hour's pleasant walk from Oakham) you may meet someone who insists that the cheese ought to be called Withcote cheese. If you visit another Leicestershire village. Wartnaby, you may meet someone who insists that the cheese ought to be called Wartnaby cheese because it was first made by a Wartnaby woman, Mrs Murson or Musson, wife of a local farmer. A fourth tradition says that the cheese was invented by the housekeeper at Quenby Hall, who eventually moved to Stilton.

Historians now believe that Stilton cheese was first made during the second or third decade of the eighteenth century, at one or other of three Leicestershire villages: Wymondham, Dalby, Quenby. Although the historians can neither prove nor disprove a fifth tradition, that the inventor was a Mrs Stilton (sometime head dairymaid at Belvoir Castle), nobody denies that the cheese was made popular by a Mrs Paulet of Wymondham, who sold large quantities of it to a relative, Cooper Thornhill, landlord of the Bell Inn at Stilton, who in turn sold it to travellers who recommended it to their friends. No matter what its origin, Stilton cheese is still made in the district, though the processes have been modified, and one doubts that any gourmet now shares the experience of Daniel Defoe: 'Stilton', he wrote, 'a town famous for cheese, which is call'd our English Parmesan, and is brought to table with mites, or maggots on it, so thick, that they bring a spoon with them for you to eat the mites with, as you do the cheese.'

Few people have heard of Aughton; fewer still of Aughton Pudding. The place is a riverside village between Gressingham and Lancaster, not to be confused with another Lancashire Aughton, a few miles from Ormskirk. In 1824 two Aughton men, William and Robert Lamb, earned their living by making baskets from willows which they boiled before peeling. When someone suggested that the boiler could be used to make a gigantic pudding, the Lambs agreed, and a communal feast was enjoyed by the villagers. From time to time a few more Aughton Puddings were made, but none has equalled the pudding of 1866, whose ingredients included 300 lbs of dried fruit, 150 lbs of sugar, 100 lbs of flour, 900 eggs, ten gallons of milk, and three gallons of rum. Weighing several hundredweights, the pudding was boiled continuously for five days and nights. A local newspaper reported that eight thousand people attended the Aughton Feast and were served by waiters from Lancaster. Their digestion was either improved or impaired by the excitement of watching running races that had been specially arranged for the occasion.

The Welsh rarebit is a corruption of Welsh rabbit, first recorded in 1725. The dish, however, must be at least as old as a tenth-century law of Hywel Da, decreeing that the palace doorkeeper should 'have the remains of the cheese he shall toast'. In 1622 'cob' was a dialect word for a lump of bread, whence Dorset cob. Dumplings probably took their name from an old Germanic word, *dump*, meaning 'damp'. The phrase 'Norfolk dumpling' may have been coined by someone who supposed that Norfolk people were short and stout, i.e. dumpy. The connection between a place and a product is sometimes tenuous. Aylesbury, for example, is in Buckinghamshire, yet when I asked a waiter whether he recommended the Aylesbury duckling, he replied: 'Certainly. It comes direct from the boss's farm in Sussex.'

Defying the Elements

There are days when a countryman sits by the fire, listening to the wind and rain. If he does bestir himself to take a walk, it is more for the dog's sake than his own; and in the end he may need to bestir the dog also. Few creatures are more perverse than a dog that is reluctant to go for the walk on which his master has reluctantly taken him. In old dogs this valetudinarianism is excusable; in young ones it is exasperating. My own dog shows no such reluctance. I have seen him rush from the house into a snowdrift, and from the stable into a gale that would have grounded the Valkyrie. Come rain, come shine—come anything that has yet been recorded in the annals of the British climate—Jack will be there and more than there . . . he will be halfway down the drive, or over the wall and into the wood.

Although we are well aware that Nature does not suffer moods, and that a stormy sky is no more likely to presage national disaster than a blue sky is likely to precede personal deliverance, still we remain affected by the weather. Most of us would rather be married on a sunny morning in May than on a foggy afternoon in November. Meanwhile, having started out, the reluctant countryman decides that—moody or not—the weather certainly depresses his own opinion of it. The sky is neither clear and cordial nor tumultuous and majestic; it is grey and low and cold and damp. The east wind comes straight out of Russia, bringing the kind of ruthlessness which we expect from that quarter. Fallen branches litter the lane. Dead leaves lose their lustre, sodden and shrivelled. Invisible behind a drystone wall, sheep cough, sounding eerily like a case of human bronchitis. Cows stare over gates, looking as though they are chewing a comfortless cud. Prodding a hedge with his stick, the walker uncovers a desiccated blackberry and a wren's derelict nest.

Having reached the crossroads, he remembers that he basked there in autumnal sunshine only a few weeks ago, and that in a month's time he will be there again, admiring the first snowdrop. If his walk takes place on a Sunday he may go the rounds without meeting a soul, because people who spend their working life in the open air tend to stay indoors during a wet weekend. It is townsfolk for whom the day of rest is the least restful, spent travelling in search of things which a countryman finds at home. When the contours allow, the walker may follow a route with the wind blowing him up the hill. What a relief it is when the lane enters a combe, away from that wind; but on gaining the summit the walker is greeted by barbed-wire whining and by bare trees bellowing, as in Meredith's pandemonium:

> Discords out of discords spin
> Round and round derisive din.

Sometimes the weather challenges a countryman to stretch his stroll into a genuine walk. Then indeed his intellect yields to his imagination, and he regards the elements as personal enemies, satanically seeking whom they may devour. Many an Arctic fantasy has been indulged by a man striding across the wintry Quantocks, or from Hawes to Tan Hill. After half an hour of sleet-stung cheeks, he likens himself to the gallant Captain Oates. The four miles still separating him from his home become an infinite expanse of inescapable hazards, and he sees himself lying exhausted in a field, watched over by a faithful dog. After an hour's plodding into a gale, the wish to achieve an appetite for tea changes into the need to satisfy it. As G. M. Trevelyan remarked, hungry walkers soon discover that 'food and drink become subjects for epic celebrations'. With half a mile still to go, the walker decides that he will have two boiled eggs, not one, and six slices of toast instead of four. When at last he does sight his house he feels as though he had marched twenty miles on an empty stomach. Entering, he says; 'Is tea ready?'

E. V. Lucas, a great walker in Sussex, held strong views about toast. 'The butter,' he insisted, 'must drench. It thus becomes gloriously indigestible.' Such succulence will horrify our own health-haunted era, but most people eighty years ago took more exercise than we do, and were therefore less likely to suffer an attack of Progress. Mrs Gamp was another who held strong views about toast, declaring that it must never be served without first 'cutting off the crusts, in consequence of tender teeth, and not too many of 'em.'

Bread, by the way, should be toasted manually, not mechanically, for whereas machines obey strict rules, a toasting fork resembles a conductor's baton in that the procedure can be modified instantly. It has, so to say, second thoughts, and is able to express them. With a flick of the wrist it can embrown a pallid patch, or rescue the crust from incineration. In short, a fork will toast bread according to the toaster's predilections, not according to the manufacturer's instructions; and it never breaks down.

Should anyone protest that buttered toast has nothing whatever to do with walking in wild weather, I confute him stating that my own thoughts on the subject occurred while I was battling against a gale near the moorland parish of High Bray in the county of Devon.

For Better and For Worse

It would indeed be difficult to over-praise the boons which technology has bestowed on country life. Only the other afternoon I found myself within a mile of a farmhouse I had not seen since I stayed there as a paying guest during the 1930s. On learning that the farmer was still alive, I decided to renew an old acquaintance. Arriving, I noticed that the yard, formerly a quagmire, was cobbled and clean. The milk shed—a damp and draughty den, permanently flanked with dung, where the farmer milked six cows—had been transformed. The floor was paved, the walls were whitewashed, the conduits were rinsed, and the milking machine shone like a chef's kitchen.

After staring politely, the farmer and I recognized each other, but instead of recalling the good old days we began to admire the better new ones, not least because an operation on the farmer's hip had lately relieved him of ten years' painful invalidism. He was, he said, a widower nowadays, but—he suddenly called: 'You there, Patty?'—his daughter and her husband had moved in to keep an eye on him. When Patty appeared we all went into the kitchen, which was warmer than the Sunday-best parlour; and what another transformation! Instead of drawing water from a pump in the yard, as her mother had done, Patty turned on a tap. The sink that I remembered was narrow and shallow; the one that I saw was wide and deep. Although I regretted the disappearance of the open hearth, I agreed that an oil-fired stove was more convenient and did not require a sooty kettle on a rusty chain. I preferred the old two-valve radio to the new coloured television, and I was sorry that oil lamps and candles had been supplanted by tubes of harsh light; even so, the blemishes seemed bearable when I went to wash my hands before tea, not at the kitchen sink but in the old larder, which now contained a bath and WC, suggesting that the family no longer retired to a privy behind the barn.

'In the old days', I reminded them, 'you went to market in a trap. Now, I see, you've got a Land-Rover.'

'Must keep up with the times,' the veteran replied.

'The tradesmen,' I remembered, 'wouldn't call here in those days. They said it was too remote, and the track too rough.'

'Ah, but we've a metalled road now. In fact, Jacksons call every Tuesday.'

'Do they,' I asked, 'still sell everything?'

'Almost,' said Patty. 'We can buy bread, cakes, groceries, fruit, vegetables, sausages, pies, and pretty well all we need for the kitchen . . . polish, dusters, soap flakes, and so forth. But as Dad said, Jacksons come to *us* nowadays, instead of us having to go to them. And what a journey it was, especially in winter. A mile of mud, then a mile of potholes, and then Percy Goodwin's sheep straying all over the place.'

'They've a cattle-grid now,' the farmer said. 'Least, the son has. Poor old Perce passed on thirty years ago. And that's another thing, 'cause when Perce were a nipper the farm burned down afore the brigade arrived. But last September, when his son fired the stubble, the brigade was up less than twenty minutes after he'd phoned 'em. Just think o' that . . . along all those lanes and through all these mountains. And we've a mobile library, too. It's got the best collection of blood-and-thunder I've ever seen.'

'They do have other things,' Patty pointed out. 'Last week my eldest boy borrowed a book about herbs and such. The pictures were smashing. Anyway, Dad doesn't always choose blood-and-thunder. I've often seen him reading books about bee-keeping.'

'Does the library stop at the crossroads?' I asked.

Patty glanced at her father. 'As a matter of fact,' she revealed, 'they kindly come as far as our gate. You see, there's a writer living hereabouts—in Aunt Emma's old cottage, actually—and on library days he stands at the crossroads and says to people, "You're reading my livelihood without paying me". It doesn't seem a nice way of going on. If he objects to people reading his books without paying him, why does he bother to write?'

Then the telephone rang, announcing that the children would be late because the school bus had broken down. 'I'm glad we're on the phone,' the old man remarked. 'But Patty and her brothers always walked to school, and I can't see it's done 'em any harm. Patty's not been ill since the mumps thirty years ago.'

'Thirty years ago,' Patty replied, 'walking was different.'

'Different? How?'

'It was safe then. You don't suppose I'd let my little Jenny go wandering round the lanes? Everyone's got a car now. You never know who you'll meet.'

'Yes,' the farmer sighed, 'I see what you mean. And in those years we didn't have yellow lines painted all down the village street. But we did have a policeman. Ah, and we had a parson, too. Our own parson, not somebody else's curate.'

That set me thinking, and my meditation was jolted when they told me that Patty's elder brother had lost his job because a prolonged strike had bankrupted the factory, and that Patty's sister-in-law took sleeping tablets because low-flying aircraft kept her awake at nights. Nor was that all. The nearest callbox had been vandalized; the church was locked against thieves; and the landlord of The Wheatsheaf recently spent three weeks in hospital, having been attacked by youths from a town twenty miles away. All in all, I felt thankful that Progress had not yet exacted quite such a heavy price from my own part of the world.

On the Eve

The door of a country house opens and a venerable cleric wheels his bicycle onto the drive. 'Where's that boy?' he calls. The boy (nowadays an elderly man) is the cleric's grandson. He duly appears, likewise wheeling a bicycle, with a woollen scarf wrapped round his Eton collar. Then the pair proceed down a lane, their lamps casting yellow pools on frosty hedges and the faces of ruminant sheep. Presently the sound of church bells is heard; only two bells, yet to the retired clergyman they seem as memorable as the peal that Robert Bridges heard on Christmas Eve:

It was starry music,
Angels' song, comforting
As the comfort of Christ
When he spake tenderly
To his sorrowful flock.

Now the cyclists overtake a man on foot, who says: 'Evening, Sir. I see you've brought your own congregation.' In fact, the cleric is himself a member of the congregation, and, like the pedestrian, he soon turns from the lane onto a track.

'What is that star?' he asks, pointing with a gloved forefinger.

'Sirius?' the child suggests.

'In your astronomy every star is Sirius. Never mind. You may still have seventy years in which to discover the Pole.'

By this time a third cyclist has arrived, followed by three people in a pony and trap, muffled and gloved, all making for the church. At last the lamplit windows are seen, stained-glass against the darkness. Beyond them the track ends at a stream, and beyond the stream stands the Hall, hidden among trees. It is cold inside the church. Even when the door has been shut, a wind whistles through, flickering the candles and swaying the oil lamps. There are about forty worshippers, chiefly farmfolk, who walk respectfully past a cushioned pew containing the squire and a horsey spinster from the Hall. A girl at the harmonium coughs nervously when the priest enters from the vestry. Then, in a scholarly voice, the priest imprints indelible words on the child's memory: 'Dearly beloved, the Scripture moveth us in sundry places to acknowledge and confess our manifold sins and wickedness . . .' From time to time the congregation sings unto the Lord a very old song indeed, harkening to the herald angels, or bidding the faithful come joyfully and in triumph to Bethlehem. So the liturgy unfolds, moving sonorously from alpha to omega: 'Fulfil now, O Lord, the desires and petitions of thy servants, as may be most expedient for them.' The child himself is uncertain to what extent the Almighty really did vouchsafe the promised Christmas gift of a three-speeding bicycle.

Many children have heard Evensong at a country church, and although in later life they may reject the dogma, nearly all of them are grateful to have been bred thereon, for without a knowledge of it none can drink deeply of our cultural heritage. Moses and the bulrushes, Daniel and the lions, Judas and the silver . . . those are passwords, distinguishing a true from a merely commercial education. King James's Bible and Thomas Cranmer's Prayer Book have merged with Greece and Rome to mould much that is finest in English literature.

Meanwhile, in an icy porch, the worshippers come down to earth. For some of them the season revives painful memories, or coincides with unexpected sorrow, yet the general mood is of sober optimism. 'Them rheumatics any better, Ben?' . . . 'I told 'im straight, if only you'd get your tyres pumped up you wouldn't need to walk so much' . . . 'Katie, gal, I reckon you've got that old 'armonium under control at last, 'cept when it 'icupped during the Nunc Dimy-titis' . . . 'Goodnight, Tom' . . . 'Merry Christmas, Mary'. Now the churchwardens emerge, accompanied by young George, a radio operator on leave from the Merchant Service, to whom the postman offers a word of advice: 'George, my lad, go easy with the cherry brandy this evening. Remember what 'appened when Jack Taylor took three for the road and then 'ad to eat 'is Christmas pudden in 'ospital.'

While the grandfather talks with the squire, the officiating priest helps an old woman into the pony and trap, saying: 'It was good of you to come, my dear. Such a cold night, too. Give my love to your husband, and say we all hope he'll be up and about again in time for his birthday next month.' Noticing George, the priest says: 'I'd be most grateful if you can call at the rectory on your way home. Our crystal set has lost its voice, I know you understand these things.' George replies with a seamanly: 'Aye, aye, Sir.'

As for the child, it cannot be his imagination when he distinctly hears the squire mutter to the spinster: 'By God, it was cold in there. Feels as if we're due for a blasted blizzard.

Why the devil they don't use more coke . . . ah, good evening, rector. I was just saying to Miss Compton-Varney, it feels as if we're due for some manna from Heaven.'

'Deep and crisp and even, eh? Well, a white Christmas would certainly please my small daughter.'

After a few more seasonable greetings the retired clergyman beckons his grandson, and together they wheel their bicycles onto the track. One by one, or in small groups, the faithful make their way home, glad that they came out, and not less glad that they will soon go in to a blazing hearth and all the trimmings of Christmas in the country.